Some Action of Her Own

Some Action of Her Own

The Adult Woman and Higher Education

Edited by

Helen S. Astin
University of California,
Los Angeles

Lexington Books
D.C. Heath and Company
Lexington, Massachusetts
Toronto   London

Library of Congress Cataloging in Publication Data

Main entry under title:

Some action of her own.

    Bibliography: p.
    Includes index.
    1. Higher education of women—Addresses, essays, lectures. 2. Adult education of women—Addresses, essays, lectures. I. Astin, Helen S.
LC1671.S65   376'.65   75-43476
ISBN 0-669-00567-3

Published simultaneously in Canada

Printed in the United States of America

International Standard Book Number: 0-669-00567-3

Library of Congress Catalog Card Number: 75-43476

Contents

Preface   vii

Acknowledgments   xi

Part I   *Continuing Education for Women: History and
                Programs*   1

Chapter 1   **The Birth of an Idea: An Account of the Genesis
                of Women's Continuing Education**   *Elizabeth L.
                Cless*   3

Chapter 2   **The Case-Study Programs: Academic Misfits
                Which Lasted**   *Carole Leland*   23

Part II   *Women and Their Families*   43

Chapter 3   **Adult Development and Education**   *Helen S.
                Astin*   45

Chapter 4   **A Profile of the Women in Continuing
                Education**   *Helen S. Astin*   57

Chapter 5   **Home Life of Women in Continuing
                Education**   *Joseph Katz*   89

Part III   *What the Future Holds*   107

Chapter 6   **Women's Continuing Education: Whither
                Bound?**   *Jessie Bernard*   109

                Epilogue   125

Appendix A   **Sample and Procedures**   131

Appendix B   **Historical Notes on the American Council on
                Education's Involvement with the Concerns of
                Women in Higher Education**   139

Appendix C   **Frequency Distributions**   147

                References   167

                Index   175

                About the Contributors   181

                About the Editor   183

Preface

Even before Margaret Mead and Betty Friedan rebuked them for their return to the cave, women in the 1960s were beginning to return to academia. The eighteen-year-olds had few problems; they could enter by the front gate with no questions asked. But their older sisters could not. If they wanted to resume their education after having taken time out to bear and rear children, they found the gates of the established institutions closed to them.

These adult women needed help. Fortunately a few dedicated leaders recognized and responded to this need. They saw access to higher learning *not* as the exclusive prerogative of the young but as the right of all able and motivated adults. They felt that academic structures should not be carved in stone but rather should be able to accommodate a wide range of students. Gradually, they learned how to bend these structures to serve returning women. Once the way had been pioneered, women of all races and from all social classes followed the new path, eager to get a piece of the academic action.

This book was designed to give an analytic account of the development of programs of continuing education for women (CEW), of the impact of these programs on the lives of the women they serve, and their influence on the institutions which house them and on higher education in general. The study was originally designed to deal with five major areas of inquiry:

1. *Demographic and background characteristics.* What are the demographic characteristics of women in continuing education programs? What are their ages, racial/ethnic backgrounds, socioeconomic circumstances, educational and occupational development, and marital and family status? Have the kinds of women who enroll in CEW programs changed over time and, if so, what are the trends? What are the counseling, educational, and personal needs of mature women returning to school and work? What are the obstacles and problems they face?

2. *Program structure and components.* How have the various CEW programs developed? How have they evolved programmatically to accommodate the specialized needs of the populations they serve? What lessons can we learn from these efforts—which represent the most innovative approaches in higher education—with respect to existing institutional structures?

3. *Impact of the program on the parent institution.* What are the elements of the relationship between the program and the parent institution? Do the programs occupy a place of prominence, or are they peripheral? What are the interests of administrators at the parent institution with respect to the program? Do they provide support and, if so, in what ways? What

have administrators and faculty learned about adult learners and their needs from experience with the CEW programs? Are they beginning to allow more flexibilities in programs and structures within the larger institutions?

4. *Impact of programs on women themselves.* What impact have various program components had on the lives of the women they serve? In what ways have the educational progress and aspirations, occupational status and plans, and personal growth of these women been directly affected by their experiences in the programs?

5. *Impact on the family.* What are the family's perceptions of and attitudes toward the wife and mother who returns to school or work? What changes are taking place in the family that permit these women to assume new responsibilities and to synergize new roles with those they have been performing in the past?

Other specific questions that arose as we began the study and continued through its various phases were:

- Given the financial and psychic investment they require, have the programs been worth it? If so, in what ways?
- What have we learned about the needs, life styles, and development of adults after fifteen years of experience with programs of continuing education for women?
- How have the basic differences and conflicts between program directors (who are client-oriented) and institutional administrators (who are institution-oriented) been handled or resolved?
- What are the roles of men—husbands, professors, employers—in the lives of these women? Are they supportive? Do they understand the needs of the returning adult women? Can they be enlightened and assisted in developing a greater appreciation of the interests and goals of adult women in continuing education programs?
- What are the structural and administrative strains in the programs? How can they best be alleviated?

The study sample includes fifteen CEW programs selected to represent the diversity of existing programs: rural versus urban settings, community colleges versus four-year institutions, coed versus primarily single-sex institutions, sectarian versus nonsectarian support, mixed versus homogeneous populations, state versus institutional bases, and large, multifaceted programs versus small, single-focus ones. The programs in the study were: Center for Continuing Education, Sarah

Lawrence College; Minnesota Women's Center, University of Minnesota; Continuing Education for Women, University of Minnesota; Women's Center for Continuing Education, University College, Syracuse University; Center for Continuing Education and Special Academic Programs, The Claremont Colleges; Human Development and Services, University Extension, University of California at Los Angeles; Center for Continuing Education of Women, University of Michigan; Center for the Continuing Education of Women, Miami-Dade Community College; Continuing Education for Women Center, George Washington University; Continuing Education for Women, University of Pittsburgh; Women's and Out-state Programs, Extension Division, University of Missouri - St. Louis; The Radcliffe Institute; Division of Continuing Education, Mundelein College; Continuing Education Programs for Women, Oregon State System of Higher Education; Division for Continuing Education, University of Missouri - Kansas City.

The first phase of the study called for case studies of each of the fifteen continuing education programs for women. The case studies were conducted through site visits, during which in-depth interviews were held with administrators in the parent institution, with the program's director and staff, and with women who had participated or were participating in the program. Spouses and children were also interviewed.

The second phase of the study included a mail survey of 1,000 current participants, 300 of their spouses, and 1,000 alumnae from the fifteen programs. (For more details on the sample and procedures see Appendix A.)

The first part of this book sketches a framework in which to examine continuing education for women. In the first chapter, Elizabeth Cless, one of the early leaders in continuing education, gives a historical account of the CEW movement, analyzing those sociocultural factors in the 1950s that first led educators to consider the problem of the education of adult women, describing early experimental programs and the women responsible for their establishment, and indicating the present status of such programs and their probable future development.

Spurred by the pioneering efforts described in the first chapter, many institutions took up the challenge of providing meaningful educational opportunities for adult women returning to education. In Chapter 2, Carole Leland looks at CEW programs in the context of the higher education institutions that house them. She characterizes the fifteen programs used as case studies in the present investigation: their genesis, funding, components and services, faculty and staff, relation to the parent institution, as well as their perceived successes and problems. The story is far from complete. The question remains: Will more institutions awaken to the needs—and the considerable potentialities—of adult women and develop programs for them? What effects will those programs have on their parent institutions? Will other groups benefit from the break-throughs made by women's continuing education?[a]

But the book is about more than programs and institutions. In Part II, we turn our attention to the women themselves and to their families, presenting both the empirical findings and the personal impressions that emerged from our study of the women in the programs and their husbands and children.

Chapter 3 sets the stage for this analysis, drawing on three sources of literature: adult development, adult education, and continuing education for women.

The demographic characteristics of women in CEW, their educational and occupational status and aspirations, their self-concepts and attitudes, and their experiences in the programs are discussed in Chapter 4. Also in this chapter are the results of some special analyses designed to elucidate the factors related to such outcomes as enrolling in a degree or certificate program, having a high degree of career commitment, and expressing satisfaction with the CEW program.

In Chapter 5, Joseph Katz paints a vivid picture of the home lives of the married women in our sample, and specifically of the reactions of their husbands and children to their return to higher education. Family relationships—mutual respect and supportiveness as well as anxieties and tensions—are discussed.

Part III looks to the future. Jessie Bernard, with support and assistance from the Advisory Committee to the study, discusses demographic trends that may play a role in the future education of women and presents three different scenarios based on these trends. She also teases out some of the subtler implications of CEW.

The Epilogue provides a brief overview of the major findings with a strong recommendation for institutional changes that would permit access of adult women to higher education and assure progress and attainment of their goals.

Helen S. Astin

---

[a]Women's continuing education, the major concern of this study, is only one aspect of the many-pronged attack now being made on women's educational problems: other aspects are women's centers and women's studies, both of which are worthy of serious study. It is to be hoped that they will also receive research attention, but to include them in this study would be diversionary.

Acknowledgments

This project had the support and assistance of many people. First, we would like to thank the National Coalition for Research on Women's Education and Development, particularly Elizabeth Cless who was its president during the first year of the project and Jean O'Barr, current president. It was the Coalition that suggested the idea for a study of continuing education for women and asked me to develop a proposal and direct the study if it got funded. Florence Anderson of the Carnegie Corporation was instrumental in our receiving the grant from the Corporation.

Joseph Katz and Carole Leland served as project associates and were intimately involved in the data collection during the case-study phase of the project.

We would like to thank the interviewers who assisted during this phase of the study: Margaret Baker, Sue Bolman, Marta Brockmeyer Brown, Marylyn Burns, Barbara Dorset, Myra Fabian, Karen Farber, Pearl Franzblau, Elizabeth Greene, Kay Hartshorn, Jacqueline Kosh, Marjorie Lozoff, Ann Marcus, Elaine Meisner, Kathleen Merrill, and Patricia Stickney.

Of course, the directors of the CEW programs and their staffs were instrumental in identifying the samples for us and helping us at every step along the way by making contact with the women and their families and by providing space for the interviews.

Doris Lorentzen, at the Radcliffe Institute, served as our financial officer, arranged two of our advisory committee meetings, and assisted in the logistics of the case study data collection.

Special thanks go to my support team at UCLA. In the initial stages, Allison Parelman, a graduate student in psychology, served as a research intern, and her assistance in the formulation of interview and survey questions as well as in interview data collection is greatly appreciated.

Patty McNamara and Yvonne Guy, both graduate students in counseling, were the research assistants, working on all aspects of the project: formulating questions, collecting data, carrying out analyses, and writing sections of the first draft. Joy McCaslin, the project secretary, helped enormously in coordinating the efforts of the many persons involved. She also typed the many drafts of the report and the final version.

Throughout the study we had the expert advice of Jessie Bernard, Esther Raushenbush, Allan Cartter, and Matina Horner, who served as members of the project's advisory committee. We appreciate their assistance.

Laura Kent, the editor, went through each chapter, accommodating to each author's individual style in order to develop a coherent manuscript.

Our appreciation and thanks go to all the participants and especially to the women and their families who so generously gave of their time and provided numerous insights into the role of continuing education programs in their development.

Part I
Continuing Education for Women: History and Programs

1

The Birth of an Idea: An Account of the Genesis of Women's Continuing Education

Elizabeth L. Cless

History confirms the fact that whenever woman is valued solely as an object to satisfy man's desires and bear his children, with no personal value of her own apart from these at best transitory abilities, her position in society is on a level with any other movable chattel and the type of education meted out to her, if any, is just such as is required to train her for her slavery to man.

Mary Wollstonecraft in 1768? John Stuart Mill in 1857? Betty Friedan in 1963? Gloria Steinem in 1970? No, this statement was made by an Assistant Professor of Philosophy and Theology at a small Midwestern Catholic college in that most unfeminist of periods, 1957 [Furlong, 1957].

Indeed, 1957 was a watershed year for American higher education: On October 4, the Soviet Union launched Sputnik, the first artificial earth satellite; in the midst of widespread material prosperity, the United States suddenly found itself intellectually poor. Sputnik caused a flurry in the dovecotes of academia. Words like "brainpower," "manpower," and "womanpower" were pushed into academic thinking by a Labor Department that found the nation overstocked on muscles and under-stocked on minds. Despite an alltime high in college and graduate school enrollments, professional, technical, and managerial ranks were dangerously thin. Though men were entering these fields in numbers closely related to their college and professional school enrollments, women were not. Findings like those of Robert L. Sutherland (Director of the Hogg Foundation for Mental Hygiene at the University of Texas and one of the original members of the American Council on Education's Commission on the Education of Women) were widely circulated in colleges and universities. Dr. Sutherland reported:

1. The number of women in the United States exceeds the number of men by over one million; by 1960 the difference is expected to reach two million.

2. The proportion of high-ability women students continuing their education beyond high school is lower than that of men, and the differential increases at each successive level of education. About half of the brightest 40 percent of high school graduates go on to college, and of the half that stay away, two-thirds are women. Of those who go on to college, the women drop out at a faster rate, leaving only 37 percent who graduate in contrast to 55 percent of the men. . . .

1

3. Our population is increasing faster than ever, yet women get through with the job of rearing children younger than ever before and have time, not children, on their hands for more years than did either their ancestors or any other women in the modern world. . . .

4. The trend toward younger marriages and earlier families means that women have less opportunity to acquire education or skill-training in their twenties [Sutherland, 1959, pp. 14–15].

For the most part, women seemed unaware of the pattern sketched by Sutherland. Feminism was equated with the struggle for suffrage, something past and faintly ludicrous. By 1950, more American women than ever before had had some college experience, but most of them had married and produced children as early and as fast as possible. This pattern persisted through the early postwar years, resulting in a highly personal and isolated world for women. Settled in suburbia, supposedly living the "good life," caught up in the "togetherness" so highly touted by the women's magazines, the American woman (with certain glaring exceptions) was enjoying the highest standard of living yet known. But the patio barbecues, the television sets, the dishwashers, and all the other trappings of affluence did not, it seems, automatically produce happiness. Later, Betty Friedan was to label this dissatisfaction among American women "the problem that has no name." Some women tried to relieve their discontent by taking jobs, only to find that the explosion of knowledge had rendered their former skills and education obsolete; as a result, their only access was to jobs at salaries that no man would consider.

Marriage was still the major goal of young women, even though the divorce rate was moving perceptibly upward. The single woman was viewed as a pitiful victim, not as an agent of choice. Sutherland reported that the average age for first marriage dropped from twenty-two in 1890 to twenty in 1950, with 1.4 percent of this decline occurring between 1940 and 1950. So prominent was the view of marriage as the ultimate good, that in 1955 Esther Lloyd-Jones defined the important question not as how to encourage women to defer marriage until they had finished college, but as how best to adapt educational resources to meet the needs of women, given the changed biological and social pattern of their lives. If marriage was encroaching on the college years, she said, perhaps the education of women should assume a different pattern from that of men. A few years later Mary I. Bunting made a similar suggestion:

Precious little attention has been given to designing educational opportunities to meet the needs of married women. Rather, we have assumed that she is not interested in continuing her education. The possibility that the choice could be a question of timing rather than goals has not received serious attention.[a]

It is interesting to note that both these women who questioned the traditional male-oriented timing of higher education were among the many distinguished people who composed the Commission on Women's Education of the American Council on Education (ACE) in the late 1950s. That Commission was the seedbed of a radical but undervalued movement for educational reform that became known as continuing education for women (CEW).

The Beginnings: ACE's Commission on the Education of Women

In the early 1950s, American colleges and universities were beginning to explore some of the issues and problems connected with the education of women. That exploration was guided by the American Council on Education, under the leadership of President Arthur Adams. As early as 1919, three years after it was founded, ACE had appointed a Committee on Training Women for the Professions and had worked quietly since that time to broaden educational opportunity for women. But not until 1951 did it "especially identify women's education as a distinct part of the education of man and as an area of the Council's active concern" [Allen, 1959]. *Women in the Defense Decade,* the published proceedings of an ACE conference held in 1951, had recommended that a standing committee on the subject be established within ACE. The next year, the annual meeting of the National Association of Women Deans and Counselors centered on the question of "whether women faculty and students were working at the height, depth and breadth of their capacities" [Allen, 1959]. Then, in 1953, ACE's standing committee and the Deans came together, and, "after careful investigation . . . as to the validity of the concerns surrounding women's education" [Allen, 1959], they formed the Commission on the Education of Women. A number of prominent people—from business, politics, and the arts as well as from academe—gave impetus and direction to research on the woman student, periodically bringing together researchers and educators to review past and current investigations and to develop suggestions for new studies.

After examining Department of Labor statistics, research on occupational choice and personality development, and studies of alumnae, the Commission reached two then-revolutionary conclusions: first, that the timetable and expectations inherent in traditional higher education for men do not necessarily call forth the best intellectual efforts of women

---

[a]The academic women whose pioneering efforts are discussed here were asked to provide an "oral history": i.e., a tape recording of their answers to five specific questions on the initiation and development of the programs with which they were connected. Many complied with this request; others gave their answers in written form, often with accompanying documentation in the form of memoranda and so forth. Many of the quoted passages in this chapter are based on that oral or written material.

students or prepare them for the demands of later life; second, that a shared female biological pattern does not justify imposing a shared female educational pattern. The female half of our population is not a homogeneous group. The curricular needs of a female doctor are similar to those of a male doctor and very different from those of a female or male professor of Romance languages. In 1975, these are not startling statements; in 1959 they were disturbing to male and female traditionalists alike. For almost a century, women in four-year colleges had been confined to two generally acceptable tracks: a liberal arts curriculum devoid of preprofessional emphasis (except for isolated programs for elementary school teaching) or a home economics program that covered "(1) preparation for homemaking, (2) preparation for related professions, (3) education for community participation, and (4) general education for personal development" (LeBaron, 1959). Both options demanded four years of uninterrupted study and in most cases were open only immediately after high school graduation.

The Commission challenged these traditional notions with the publication of *How Fare American Women?* in 1959 and *The Span of a Woman's Life and Learning* in 1960. Without the solid base of research on women undertaken and given wide circulation by the Commission in the 1950s, the new patterns of women's education now loosely grouped under the heading of continuing education for women would not have come into being. Margaret Habein Merry, a long-time member of the Commission, seized on the idea—implicit or explicit in much of that research—that women's education might profitably have a pattern different from men's education. Her encouragement, and the practical help given by Opal David, the Commission's director from 1958 to 1961, were sustaining supports for the three initial experiments—at the University of Minnesota, Radcliffe, and Sarah Lawrence—in changing the traditional forms of education for women.

In 1963, ACE published *Education and a Woman's Life,* the proceedings of the 1962 Itasca conference, convened to explore the strength of this new pattern in higher education. Previously, just as plans for the conference were being made, the Commission on the Education of Women was suddenly dissolved during a reorganization of Council structure by Logan Wilson, Arthur Adams's successor as president of ACE. The minutes of the October 4, 1961, meeting of ACE's Executive Committee give the following explanation:

The President of the Council reported that the Commission on the Education of Women had been discontinued because funds are not available for further operations.

He further reported that the members of the Commission have been invited to serve on a Committee for the Conference on the Continuing Education of

Women. A grant from the Carnegie Corporation will make possible a conference on this subject in the summer of 1962. The Committee will continue up to and through the conference with responsibilities for conference planning.

As far as available records show, the matter was not discussed further. (See Appendix B for a more detailed discussion of ACE's involvement with the concerns of women in higher education.)

It was 1973 before Roger Heyns, Wilson's successor at ACE, reestablished the Commission (now called the Commission on Women in Higher Education). The resulting twelve-year hiatus in official concern about the problems of women in higher education had profound and predictable results. Since ACE is the largest and most inclusive association in American higher education, with leadership provided primarily by the presidents of well-known and prestigious institutions, its official neglect of academic women during the 1960s fueled the emerging feminist movement. ACE's encouragement of research on women's education during the 1950s and the supportiveness of its Board for Commission-inspired experiments in women's education had created a climate of hope and positive action. The disbanding of the Commission was seen as overt rejection by the male establishment of women faculty and of women students. It is no accident that the earliest and most unremitting pressure groups in the women's movement of the twentieth century comprised academic women, nor that the initial leadership of that movement came from middle-class women who had been to college.

The Matrix

In the 1950s the number of women who held managerial positions in business or industry was exceedingly small; the proportion of women in the professions requiring graduate training had declined markedly from the 1920s. It was distressingly obvious to the Women's Bureau of the U.S. Department of Labor that women were not going on to graduate or professional school after college or entering business and industry with any commitment. Equally disturbing in light of the country's need for brainpower, more than half of clearly identifiable able women were not giving priority to higher education during young adulthood. Explanatory statistics were available: in 1890 the average woman had her last child when she was thirty-two years old, in 1950 when she was twenty-six. It was predicted in 1957 that, within the next few years, one out of two married women would be sending her youngest child to first grade when she was only thirty-two, the age at which *her* mother was having *her* youngest child. According to demographers, the woman of the 1950s would then live on for approximately fifty more years—years empty of intense family preoccupation.

Three very different academic institutions were ready to take Esther Lloyd-Jones's suggestion that, instead of trying to encourage women to defer marriage until after college, higher education should try to adapt itself to meet the changed needs of women. These three institutions were not the only ones involved, but for a number of reasons the programs they established became the most visible and provided the impetus for others to follow their lead. The University of Minnesota established the Minnesota Plan for the Continuing Education of Women in 1960. Radcliffe College opened the Radcliffe Institute for Independent Study in 1961. Sarah Lawrence College initiated its Center for Continuing Education in 1962.

Despite their differing methods, these three experiments had a common and clearly defined purpose. They sought not to create another system of higher education to replace the historical one, nor did they propose an alternative system; rather, they aimed to open existing systems so that their riches could be enjoyed, without struggle, without eternal requests for exceptions to rules, and also without conformity to structures and timing meant for young, unmarried, unemployed students. The common purpose was to explore every possible way of making higher education available—part-time, full-time, and recurrently—throughout a woman's life, whenever she had a reason and a desire for it. She might be a fifty-year-old widow who dropped out of high school but has the ability to do college-level work and needs a job for the first time in her life, a twenty-eight-year-old secretary whose parents could not afford the nurse's training she dreamed about, a thirty-four-year-old physicist with two children who needed time and facilities to carry out research, or "just a housewife" of forty who wanted a degree in urban planning in order to professionalize her community experience. Women's continuing education identified, even sometimes created, the curricular avenues and flexibilities of timing, location, and financial aid that would bring such goals within reach by utilizing the existing system in new ways.

The one singular creation of women's continuing education was the provision to adults of preadmission academic information and referral, a kind of educational service whose techniques differ from those of traditional student counseling.[1] The importance of such a service was demonstrated by experiments like The Radcliffe Institute. Because of its highly specialized clientele, the Institute did not expect that it would have to provide academic counseling, but found itself almost overwhelmed by women who wanted information about other ways to return to study besides that offered by the Institute. Such preadmission academic direction—based on individual goals, existing commitments, and levels of competence rather than on the hospitality of the institution providing the counseling—was one of the more radical shifts in academic structure developed by women's continuing education, one that now is widely recognized as necessary for men as well as women.

In the early efforts the term "continuing education" was often used deliberately, in the restricted sense of professional refresher education. It was meant to have clear and specific meaning: that of a return to curricular discipline designed by authoritative faculty to expand skills and to introduce newly discovered knowledge to those with previous experience in higher education at varying levels.

These early programs did not, however, offer a single solution to the problem of finding alternative patterns for educating women. Their parent institutions were not geographically related. Their initiators did not belong to the same professional groups, nor did they communicate with one another often, if at all. The single thing that bound the early programs together was a general realization that women beyond traditional college age were highly educable (perhaps more so than they had been at traditional college age) and eager to return to study. Beyond that the history of these new patterns is a history of the interest and educational philosophy of each academic woman who cajoled, bullied, or persuaded a particular institution that had the resources she valued into sponsoring one particular experimental program.

Esther Raushenbush, one of the pioneers in the academic movement known as women's continuing education, began with "faculty indifference and a garage full of old furniture." Out of these assets she shaped one of the most vital programs in the country. She now speaks of her certainty that there is one

inescapable condition for the creation of any new educational enterprise. There has to be somebody who has both the conviction and the energy to make it come to life. I doubt whether any successful women's continuing education program in the country came to effective life without some one individual convinced that it should happen and able to invest the psychic energy as well as the intelligence, knowledge, and time to make it happen. I don't think an educational program (especially one that has as many strikes against it as this one has had everywhere) can be legislated by an institution or carried out by a committee. Somebody has to believe in it, and want to do it—somebody who has some credibility to begin with, and is not easily daunted.[b]

Undergirding all the early experiments in CEW—of which Minnesota, Sarah Lawrence, and Radcliffe were the most conspicuous—was funding from the Carnegie Corporation. Academic women within institutions who were both attempting to alter higher education so that it could more effectively serve women and working out of deep personal conviction that a greater number of women could and should contribute more to

---

[b]See footnote a.

American life, found their parallel on the Carnegie Corporation staff in the person of Florence Anderson. Practical and tenacious, Ms. Anderson returned academic proposals in this field over and over again, until they were rewritten in such a way that they could stand on their own, not as imitations of other new CEW programs. Each of the early programs funded by the Carnegie Corporation had a slightly different emphasis and was designed to meet the requirements of a slightly different population. In this way, the educational needs common to all returning women students were identified, as were those that characterized only women in certain fields or with special civic and cultural goals. From the beginning she had the encouragement and support of John Gardner, Alan Pifer, and other members of the Corporation staff. An interoffice memo of April 8, 1963, explains that a decision was made in 1959 "that a central theme of the Corporation's program should be Better Use of Human Resources," with a special emphasis on womanpower: Early marriage and childbearing meant that "a large proportion of new recruits for professional and sub-professional jobs" must come from the group of women over age thirty-five. Programs were needed "to train and retrain these mature women," and to give intellectual stimulation to women between the ages of twenty and thirty-five so that they would be motivated to work or study part-time while their children were young. The memo concludes: "Much more needs to be done and [the Carnegie Corporation] can help. The very few, widely scattered, existing programs merely show what can be done." It went on to state that all institutions should participate, according to their resources.

Carnegie was the first foundation to take an active interest in this problem and had earlier supported ACE's 1957 and 1962 conferences on the education of women. Though other foundations, such as Ford and Kellogg, have sporadically supported isolated or existing programs, Carnegie saw the early programs as just a part of a whole program and has continued its support of the idea in different places and in different forms, for more than fifteen years.

The Minnesota Plan for the Continuing Education of Women

Beginning formal operation in 1960, the Minnesota Plan had potentially the largest and most heterogeneous audience. It grew from a merger of two streams of thought, from the attempts of two different groups of people to solve different but related problems of women's education.

The University of Minnesota had a long and distinguished tradition of "intellectual retreats" for technical and professional training, presented through its General Extension Division. After World War II, the fields of social work and education, with their strong component of lay leadership from the community, began increasingly to use the faculty and facilities of the University, and requests for continuing education in civic and cultural affairs were made more frequently. At the same time, the University was a leader in the continuing liberal education movement of the middle 1950s, with its concomitant development of new ways of teaching to utilize adult experience.[c]

I joined the University's General Extension Division in 1954, primarily to work with the faculty in setting up institutes or workshops in the civic, cultural, and liberal arts areas. But I also became deeply involved with the traditional professional updating institutes in so-called women's fields like social work, nurse-anaesthesiology, and elementary and secondary education. This involvement led, in 1958, to my establishing the first of several year-long liberal arts seminars for postcollege-age women as well as a shorter neighborhood seminar program designed primarily for women in community work: important elements of the Minnesota Plan.

In 1957 Virginia L. Senders joined the Psychology Department, bringing with her a proposal (which she had developed earlier at Antioch but which had not been implemented there) for a program to improve education for women of all ages. While recognizing the need for more realistic life planning by young college women, it placed even more emphasis on continuing liberal and professional study, placement, and other facilitating services to older women. The office of the Dean of Women had recently been abolished at Minnesota; but the office of the Dean of Students was well aware that women had special needs that could easily be overlooked in the absence of a special advocate. It also had a firm tradition of integrating academic and cocurricular activities that Senders' proposal could build upon. Furthermore, Senders found the University's widely known Student Counseling Bureau a willing and enthusiastic resource in the planning stages of the Minnesota Plan, as well as a significant contributor to its later success.

Not until 1958 did Virginia L. Senders and I meet to combine our efforts and become cofounders and codirectors of the Minnesota Plan for the Continuing Education of Women; I focused on new structures and timing of education for women, while she stressed a new life orientation for younger women and developed mechanisms to provide support and counseling services for women older than the "regular" undergraduates. Working together with an advisory and supervisory committee of four (soon six) university deans, we developed the Plan to function as an

---

[c]In this experiment, Minnesota was only one of many universities that drew upon the research and staff expertise of the Chicago-based Center for the Study of Liberal Education for Adults, headed by A.A. Liveright.

integrated entity. Such diverse components as child care, placement, a newsletter for members, and small scholarship awards were built into the Minnesota Plan from its beginning. A key element in Ms. Senders' program for "regular" undergraduate women was a seminar, "The Educated Woman in the United States," that was one predecessor of the women's studies programs flourishing on many campuses today.

In the middle of 1962 Senders' intense affiliation with the Minnesota Plan ended when she moved to the East Coast. She was succeeded by Vera Schletzer, then a doctoral candidate in psychology and a person with an immediate and personal understanding of the problems of women returning to study after the hiatus imposed by marriage and children. Schletzer had worked as a counselor for the Plan, and her appointment as the new Codirector and Coordinator emphasized and strengthened the consultative aspect of the program.

The Minnesota Plan brought no startling new structure to the University. Its major innovation was exploiting every resource and every flexibility that could be found or created in the existing system for the benefit of women beyond the usual college age, whether high school dropouts or distinguished postdoctoral researchers. The Plan served many of both kinds, as well as women at every academic stage in between. It opened the University to all women, and they came.

The Radcliffe Institute for Independent Study

When Mary I. Bunting became president of Radcliffe College in 1960, one of her priorities was to help intellectually able and motivated women, especially those with families, do the things they wanted to do. A microbiologist prior to her marriage, Bunting had been given laboratory facilities and a small stipend at Yale University, where her husband taught, while bearing and caring for four children. This personal experience made her eager to provide similar opportunities for other capable women. A visible result of her commitment to this objective, the Radcliffe Institute for Independent Study formally opened in 1961. Bunting's own words best express the philosophic basis of the Institute at that time: "My basic concern in 1960 was not any particular group of women (i.e., Ph.D.'s with children), but the "climate of unexpectation" that inhibited so many women from *using* their capabilities productively and tempted educators and others to think of women as bright but relatively unimportant students." If women students had been considered important, the necessary adjustments in school structures could have been made, thus encouraging and assisting these women in the fulfillment of their intellectual potential.

Constance Smith came to Radcliffe as the first Dean of the Institute and remained so until her death in 1970. She and Bunting worked so closely together that it is difficult for even their friends to tell who was responsible for what aspect of the steady expansion of the Institute. We know from Bunting that, when the Institute embraced the long-standing Radcliffe seminar program (established with Carnegie Corporation support in 1951), Dean Smith referred to the Institute as Radcliffe's continuing education program, a concept which had not occurred to Bunting originally. The seminar program paralleled Radcliffe College's own beginnings in that Harvard professors (and eventually some faculty from other area colleges) came to Radcliffe to repeat selected college courses, without credit, at times convenient for older women in the Boston area. Gradually a few of the Institute Fellows began teaching new seminars in their own fields. Under the direction of Alice K. Smith, a former Fellow and successor to Constance Smith as Dean of the Institute, a number of the seminars were granted credit toward the Harvard A.B. in Extension Studies.

In 1963 through 1964 the Radcliffe Trustees established the Institute on a permanent basis: The words "for Independent Study" were dropped from the title when the seminars were incorporated in the program and when the need for further theoretical and experimental studies relating to women's careers became apparent. Originally, the Program for Independent Study was designed only to enable women scholars and artists to carry forward independent projects—not to get further degrees, or even to attend classes unless they wished to do so for their own projects. Some lawyers and business women were accepted by the Program in the early years, as were a few physicians. These exceptions often provided the seed for new programs.

In 1966, for example, a grant from the Josiah Macy, Jr. Foundation made it possible to initiate a second experiment: the Program for Women Physicians. Over a four-year period, with the cooperation of several teaching hospitals in the area, forty-three women physicians completed internships, residencies, or other postgraduate study on a part-time, prolonged schedule. In the eyes of many, this proof that advanced medical education could be successfully undertaken on a part-time basis represents the most impressive and resonant achievement of all the Radcliffe Fellowship experiments. As another thrust in this direction, a part-time Graduate Study Program at institutions in southern New England was begun in 1967 with a grant from the Charles E. Merrill Trust. This effort, channeled through the Radcliffe Institute, attempted to change institutional policies that blocked the admission of women as part-time students and made it hard for them to get financial assistance.

New programs to help the educated woman increase her own

productivity continue to evolve at the Radcliffe Institute, even as its research on all aspects of women's lives grows in importance.

The Sarah Lawrence Center for Continuing Education

By the time Esther Raushenbush became Dean of the College at Sarah Lawrence, it had an established reputation as one of the few top-quality experimental colleges in the United States. She later resigned as Dean to return to teaching and to establish the Center for Continuing Education. She describes her interest in CEW as partially a product of conversations with alumnae and mothers of students, women who had not completed their undergraduate studies.

Raushenbush was originally attracted to Sarah Lawrence for two reasons, its deep concern with designing education that was as appropriate as possible for the individual student, and its emphasis on flexibility as opposed to the rigid requirements of most colleges. In such an atmosphere, it was possible to create a program for this new population of students that was tailored to their educational and personal needs. The initial program was part-time, although the academic requirements were the same as regular undergraduate work. Having completed four semester courses in the program, the women entered the regular undergraduate program. By then their initial anxieties about studying had been removed, they had become used to systematic study and to working with other students, and were ready for the regular program.

Sarah Lawrence's Center for Continuing Education opened in 1962. At first, it focused on women seeking the baccalaureate and later created some graduate programs.

Thus, these few very different women at three very different institutions pioneered in the search for solutions to the problem of neglect or underutilization of the intellectual potential of women; each program reflected the special interests of its initiators and was tailored to the particular character of the institution that housed it. These three programs—grouped together because of the accident of their simultaneous planning and inception—represent three different approaches to the same educational goal.[2]

Early Variations on the Theme

Given impetus by the recognition accorded the Minnesota Plan, the Radcliffe Institute, and the Sarah Lawrence Center for Continuing Education, a number of highly successful programs were started in the early 1960s. Two of them deserve mention as particularly interesting in terms of their parent institutions and their evolution.[d] The first was developed at the University of Pennsylvania, which had a long history of single-sex coordinate colleges at the undergraduate level. Virginia Henderson, who had been deeply involved in the founding of the Women's College in 1933, joined Jean Brownlee, Dean of the Women's College at the time under consideration, to establish Pennsylvania's Continuing Education program. In the early 1950s, impatient with the format of traditional male reunions, their Alumnae Association was the first in the country to seek contact with the academic life of the University and to build reunions around lectures by outstanding faculty. The resulting community interest in more regular access to the University led to presidential approval of day classes in the Women's College and in the graduate schools that were open to women in the Philadelphia area. Although all classes were open, the University's President and Provost imposed stringent guidelines: No school could have more than 10 percent of these women; their academic qualifications and commitment were to be carefully screened; and they had to pay regular tuition, prorated for part-time study. As Dean Brownlee puts it, "The University only had a certain amount of time, money, and talent, so it had to be used seriously—not wasted." Ms. Henderson had two original target groups: women who had dropped out of college at the end of two years, and professionals who wanted to write. Community interest almost immediately broadened the spectrum of students to include some one-year dropouts and a number of women who had completed degrees and were changing their fields. An intensive study of part-time jobs for women was a key part of the initial program. (The resulting book was rejected by an interested publisher because it dealt only with college women. The effort to explore and encourage part-time jobs for women throughout the country has a champion in Felice Schwartz of New York, who early put together a noninstitutional but academically supervised organization called Catalyst, focused on new employment patterns for women. Many women's continuing education programs today are affiliated with this operation.) The alumnae origins of Pennsylvania's flexibility and its responsiveness to the older woman student makes it one of the most interesting of the early programs in a university.

The University of Wisconsin took a different path. Following a 1961 speech to the Mortar Board Association by Martha Peterson (then Dean of Women at Wisconsin) in which she discussed the fledgling Minnesota

---

[d]In 1961, Rutgers initiated a Mathematics Retraining Program specifically designed for women who had previously majored in math and needed short-term refresher training for vocational reasons. This program led to other short retraining courses for female college graduates, notably the Chemistry program at Wellesley, but none of them attempted to influence accepted educational timing.

Plan, Kathryn Clarenbach (an alumna with a Ph.D. in political science who had recently returned to Madison with her family) volunteered to work with Dean Peterson and her staff to explore community interest in adapting the idea. A questionnaire sent to the wives of doctors, lawyers, and faculty members drew such overwhelming response that Clarenbach was soon appointed Assistant Dean of Women for Continuing Education. At about the same time, Wisconsin's renowned Extension Division set up its own programs of noncredit courses for older women under the supervision of Constance Threinen. On the basis of her belief that service for returning women students should be an integral part of the degree-granting part of the institution, Kathryn Clarenbach used her office to move the entire University toward greater hospitality, often running interference for individual women and successfully challenging existing ground rules that discriminated against women, and indeed against all older students. One of her most revolutionary accomplishments was the removal of the usual ban against part-time study at the graduate and professional levels (except in the case of the first year of law school). In addition, although financial aid for part-time women graduate students was virtually nonexistent at the time (with even the American Association of University Women restricting to full-time students its prestigious fellowships for graduate study by older women who intended to go into college teaching), the University of Wisconsin established the E.B. Fred Fellowships for part-time graduate study by women. These fellowships were the first step toward recognizing this essential element in the reform of institutional patterns of financial aid. They were initially funded by the Carnegie Corporation; after the Carnegie grant expired the University maintained these fellowships itself—and continues to do so.

The University of Wisconsin—which had an Extension Division that, in longstanding cooperation with the state government, reached into the everyday life of most of the state's citizens—was a natural medium for the fusion of these pioneer efforts in changing women's education and the political activism of the emerging women's movement.[e] President Kennedy's National Commission on the Status of Women, established in 1962, gave official recognition to the upgrading of women from their second-class economic, legal, and academic citizenship. It quickly spawned a number of State Commissions on the Status of Women but, as far as we know, only in Wisconsin is the Commission's office housed in the University's Office for Women's Educational Resources. Kathryn Clarenbach chaired that Commission under three governors, receiving

[e]In 1967, during a top administrative change within the University, after the Office of the Dean of Women and later that of Dean of Students had disappeared at Wisconsin, Ms. Clarenbach's staff was merged with Constance Threinen's under the Dean of Extension.

the University's enthusiastic support, consistent with its tradition of service even to people ordinarily not university-oriented. Thus, the Office for Women's Educational Resources has developed ties with such far-flung groups as Wisconsin Tribal Women, the AFL-CIO Women's Council, the Women's Political Caucus (at both state and national levels), the Equal Rights Amendment Coalition, and many others. In no other state is the bond between education and nonpartisan political action so taken for granted.

By 1965, there were approximately 100 CEW programs in the United States. Not all of them were campus-based, however, and many had only tenuous connections with their degree-granting parent institutions. Consciousness raising—an effective tool of the women's movement based in part on Maslow's concept of "self-actualization"—appealed to the many women who were seeking to free themselves from their long-socialized dependence on husband and children for identity. Some independent entrepreneurs and, regrettably, a few universities created "courses" combining simplistic self-actualization techniques with consciousness raising and labeled them "continuing education." These noncredit offerings brought in dollars and provided an easy out for those colleges and universities resistant to examining their own timing and structures in the interest of realistic education for women. This unfortunate trend was not without its positive side: Outraged women scholars, most of whom applauded the true intent of consciousness raising, have given academic legitimacy to that intent through the development of women's studies. Reexamining history, sociology, psychology, literature, and the arts to illuminate women's role and contributions in these fields, they have brought about curricular change that is far beyond anything envisioned by the pioneers of women's continuing education.

Renewed Focus on Research

At a 1967 conference of CEW leaders convened by Priscilla Jackson (Director of Oakland University's Continuum Center) and financed by the Kellogg Foundation, the damage done to this emergent segment of higher education by the lack of a formal channel for access to relevant research findings was heavily underscored. Shortly thereafter Jean Pennington of Washington University enlisted the help of the Johnson Foundation of Racine to make it possible for a small number of active researchers and program directors to meet at the Radcliffe Institute in 1968 to formulate a replacement for the former ACE Commission on the Education of Women. As a result, the National Coalition for Research on Women's Education and Development came into being. The goal of researchers and administrators alike was to encourage and disseminate research on the realities of education in women's lives. Their focus, like that of the previous ACE Commission, was a careful examination of structures and procedures in higher education as they serve women of all ages in a changing society.

Following the ACE pattern of institutional membership, the National Coalition evolved slowly. Its formative years were guided by three distinguished researchers: Anne Firor Scott as president, Joseph Katz and Esther Westervelt as codirectors.[f] Thus, by the early 1970s, research needs pertinent to the structure of women's education were again being identified, and research findings were disseminated in an organized fashion. The University of Michigan's Center for Continuing Education for Women has provided the most consistent and effective model for coordinating and distributing one institution's research to all the Coalition's members.

Simultaneously, women's studies (which may loosely be defined as research on women through the academic disciplines) have enriched the content of higher education. Catalyst, an organization established by Felice Schwartz, has since the early 1960s gathered information on the employment patterns of college-educated women outside academe. The Women's Bureau of the Department of Labor has periodically documented what women do with their education. More recently, Jacquelyn Mattfeld (1971) of Sarah Lawrence and Brown University (now President-designate of Barnard College) undertook a comprehensive analytic report on those CEW programs listed by the Women's Bureau (1968). This listing was confined to those institutions and organizations that described themselves as offering academic programs or structures "with specific concern for women" and was intended "to be illustrative rather than inclusive." In her examination of the self-descriptive entries, Mattfeld found that only 156 out of the 356 listed were identifiable as "admitting or facilitating the admission of adult women into degree programs." Of the 156, fifty-two were extension or evening programs "that had no particular interest to women." In the main, these courses that presumably showed the institution's "concern" for adult women were one- or two-year refresher, paraprofessional, or training programs in stereotypic women's fields such as nursing, elementary and secondary teaching, and dental technology; they might or might not lead to a degree or a certificate. The 104 programs listed as offering work for academic credit included all types of postsecondary institutions: state and private universities, community colleges, city colleges, parochial and private

---

[f]The National Coalition was sustained by the Johnson Foundation, the Exxon Foundation and, with the underwriting of this study, the Carnegie Corporation.

colleges, women's and coeducational institutions. Mattfeld reports: "Of 50 well-known private women's colleges and coeducational colleges only four (Jackson, Radcliffe, Sarah Lawrence and Wellesley) have centers or programs of continuing education for women. An additional five (Bryn Mawr, Goucher, Marlboro, Mills and Vassar) regularly admit older women on a part-time or full-time basis." Telephone inquiries to forty-five selective private colleges throughout the country showed that three-fourths of them never admitted adult women or did so only rarely on condition that they study full-time and pay full costs, presumably including such fees as gymnasium locker fees, student dues, etc. Eleven out of these forty-five did allow part-time study; these eleven also offered financial aid, presumably on the same basis as to dependent, younger students.

Turning to the universities, Mattfeld concluded that the larger state universities and some private ones (including Claremont University Center, Temple, Syracuse, Purdue, Loyola, and Tufts) "have established centers or opened administrative units charged with responsibility of providing counsel and services for mature women reentering the university" [1971]. Fifty-two of the sixty-five state universities or colleges (80 percent) she surveyed made such provisions, as did all fourteen private universities that replied. But "Harvard, Princeton and Yale have not followed suit" [Mattfeld, 1971].

Other facts revealed by the Mattfeld study were that only forty-four of the institutions that completed and returned questionnaires had programs "primarily or exclusively designed to take into account the characteristic life style of unemployed adult women." About two in five program directors were male; only 29 percent had faculty status; and half were new to the college or university when they assumed directorship of the program. Only thirteen programs reported trying to keep data on past or present women students continuing their education. Mattfeld reports no past or current studies of alumnae of these programs, although the five-year report on the Minnesota Plan had already been published, and the Sarah Lawrence Center and the Radcliffe Institute released their ten-year reports shortly after this study. Each of these reports included only brief descriptions of alumnae but gave a more complete profile of their present student clientele.

Mattfeld makes comparisons between her study and an earlier research report on a 1970 survey of women's higher education [Oltman, 1970] which contrasts with it sharply. Oltman received questionnaire replies from 454 of the 750 colleges and universities that were corporate members of the American Association of University Women. Although 95 percent of these respondents indicated that they "offer opportunities for mature women to complete degrees," only 44 percent had any special program for mature women, and fewer than half made adjustments in timing and class scheduling to accommodate the needs of mature married or working women. None of the responding institutions could give even approximate statistics on the number or nature of the mature women students enrolled on their campuses.

The only other major source of information on women's continuing education programs currently available is a bibliography, *Current Information Sources on the Continuing Education of Women,* [1970] compiled by the Educational Resources Information Center which maintains a Clearinghouse on Adult Education at Syracuse University. The lack of hard data and of printed primary source material makes it difficult to identify those institutions that have truly tried to create realistic opportunities—in structure, financing, and timing—for married or working women to continue their education in the mainstream of academic life. Nonetheless, the many listings in the Women's Bureau pamphlet, along with the studies by Oltman and Mattfeld, illustrate how anxious many institutions are to advertise themselves as concerned about the continuing education of mature women. Unfortunately, most administrators and faculty members have completely overlooked the implications of the term "continuing education" that led to its adoption by the early planners of these programs: namely, the provision of some kind of academic structure that recognizes the multiple responsibilities of adult women and that facilitates their return to an education in a disciplined and recognized academic setting (degree or postdegree) of high quality. Whether the distinction between the original use of the term and its later—and much looser—use remains valid for all women and for all institutions is not the question. For consumer protection—and for the protection of our much-vaunted academic integrity—the time approaches when educators and concerned public alike will demand that a truth-in-advertising label be printed clearly on every package that announces itself as "continuing education for women." Perhaps then Mattfeld's conclusion—"Clearly these programs are not considered prestigious or even central to the institutions that host them"—will no longer obtain.

Report From 1975

By 1975 not one of the pioneering programs in CEW remains the same in detail. Unchanged, however, is the rationale behind such programs: that every institution of higher education offer varied and valid options of timing and procedure adapted to the needs of different age groups; and that women of every age, as first-class citizens, have total and informed access to high-quality undergraduate, graduate, and postgraduate training.

Until these two goals have been met, continuing education programs for women will be needed to prod and to innovate.

Current financial stringencies are pinching, even strangling, many highly respected CEW programs. Almost all have been underfunded from the beginning. In light of the declining number of students in the seventeen-to-twenty-four age bracket, it is hard to understand why male administrators have cut down their support of these programs, most of which have proved their effectiveness in attracting older students. Every major report on the future of higher education published during the past five years has recognized that higher education can no longer discriminate against serious students on the basis of age. Many of the most prestigious reports—such as those of the Carnegie Commission and the Newman Task Force—have recommended that preadmission supportive academic counseling be made available to returning students without acknowledging that women's continuing education programs long ago established that pattern. The new advocates of nontraditional education seem unaware that almost every innovation they suggest has been a part of these programs for at least ten years. This tendency of academic administrators to reinvent the wheel cannot be attributed entirely to their seeming unawareness of women as students, since neither do these recent converts to the idea of the external degree look to the well-established pioneers in this area, like Goddard College and the University of Oklahoma, for help and example. But women's continuing education may be victorious, even if that victory goes unsung. The proof is there that neither the quality nor the rigor of established curricula are lost when students study part-time rather than full-time, when they drop out of formal education for several years, or when academic procedures are adapted to the multiple responsibilities of the returning student.

Too many people have taken *continuing education for women* to mean little more than a noncredit palliative for the "empty nest" syndrome, not as *education for women,* with its implication of necessary continuity. They therefore ignore the necessity of reexamining current educational practices—which, in general, still reflect the needs and goals of privileged young men—in light of the life pattern of intelligent women. Such a reexamination has little to do with radical feminism and everything to do with the higher education of both women and men. Only recently—through work-study programs, coresidential dormitory life, and the like—have colleges and universities begun to shake off the remaining influences of their monastic origins. Liberal education is struggling to redefine itself in terms of twentieth-century realities and twenty-first-century possibilities. The nineteenth-century German model on which our graduate schools are based, the model provided by the Morrill Act's mid-nineteenth-century creation of land-grant colleges and universities to serve the farmer and the emerging industrialist, both assumed a student body consisting primarily of males. Our present patterns—ranging from a smattering of the liberal arts designed to civilize the barbarous adolescent through rigorous vocational education designed to prepare the student for an occupation—were designed for a captive audience of young men subject to parental bidding, ambition, and subsidy; they were expected to go straight from high school to higher education, there to spend at least four uninterrupted years. (In *Life Styles of Educated Women,* Eli Ginzberg pointed out that this pattern may no longer be suitable even for young men, but that is not our concern here.)

That the experimental programs with which we are concerned here were designed for women older than the usual undergraduate—and received such an overwhelming response from them—dramatizes one point that the researchers of the 1950s made over and over again: Education designed for men is not equally designed for women. Beginning with Halfter's study [1962] of women over age forty-five, research has consistently indicated that mature women respond to higher education with enthusiasm, ability, and a high sense of purpose. In no society do men bear children; in most societies they do not have major responsibility for taking care of children during the first five years. Childbearing is biologically most feasible for women between the ages of sixteen and thirty, the very time for which masculine higher education is designed and in which vocational choice is encouraged. Although thousands of exceptional American women have managed to bear and raise children while getting an education and establishing a career, Department of Labor statistics indicate that it is unrealistic to expect most women to be capable of such a prodigious accomplishment.

For example, one out of thirty young men intellectually capable of earning a Ph.D. did so in 1961; one out of every three hundred women of traditional graduate school age capable of earning a Ph.D. did so (U.S. Department of Labor, National Manpower Council, 1962). The relative percentages have changed only a little since that date. The first programs that provided renewed access to higher education for mature women bore out the hypotheses of researchers that women returning to formal study will surpass their own earlier intellectual performance and move on into focused and efficient social and economic productivity. The formula for testing those hypotheses has been followed: We have found out what motivated intelligent women need, we have supplied it, and this study has observed the results.

Future historians may well find the roots of the twentieth century's women's movement in research and program efforts such as those reported in this chapter, just as nineteenth-century feminism may have grown out of the admission of women to institutions of higher education.

The difference that a century has made lies in the deliberate utilization of research—the most emphasized tradition in all of American higher education—to set the foundation for social and academic change on behalf of women.

Notes

1. For a thorough discussion of these differences, see *A Five-Year Report of the Minnesota Plan.* (Schletzer et al. 1967).

2. For the definitive demographic examination of CEW programs going beyond the limits of this report, see Jean M. Campbell, "Women Drop Back In: Educational Innovation in the Sixties," in *Academic Women on the Move* (Rossi and Calderwood, eds., 1973), pp. 93-124.

2

The Case-Study Programs: Academic Misfits Which Lasted

Carole Leland

The purpose of the case studies in this study was to collect information on a small but diverse sample of continuing education programs: how they came into being, what their original objectives were, how they have evolved in purpose and program to serve the special needs of adult women, what services they offer, how they are operated, how they are related to the parent institution, what their special problems and strengths are perceived to be, and what impact they have had.

The fifteen continuing education programs for women used in the case studies are diverse with respect to institutional setting. All but one was affiliated with a college or university, the exception being a program based in a state system of higher education in the Northwest. Two of the remaining fourteen were housed in the same institution. Thus, the sample includes thirteen parent institutions, whose characteristics are charted in Table A–1 of Appendix A.

The information in this chapter was drawn from a background information sheet which gave details of each program's history, personnel, structure, facilities, program, and clientele, and from in-depth interviews with administrators, program directors, faculty members, counselors, women participants in the CEW programs, and their husbands and children. (For further details of the methodology, see Appendix A.)

The fifteen case-study programs reflect the heritage detailed in the previous chapter—a heritage of committed, visionary leadership, societal urgencies, and substantial interest and support from the foundations. They mirror as well the middle-class, middle-age values of the pioneers, predating other more militant efforts by blacks, chicanos, and feminists in the late 1960s to "humanize" higher education. In contrast to these efforts, proponents of continuing education for women (CEW) engineered no sit-ins, offered no overt hostilities, and earned no arrest records. Though they sought change—revolutionary flexibilities and responses in academe—they carried on their effort with little fanfare and infrequent notice by their institutions, save for the few administrators who at best crusaded with them and at least did not refuse to accommodate them. What they have accomplished in little over a decade touches thousands of women in this country and may have opened institutional doors for nontraditional students—male and female—doors which were rudely closed when these programs began.

23

Today, the programs face a different decade and a different social and economic milieu. Whether colleges and universities need or can afford to keep these social agencies at their sides may be a more conclusive test of continuing education programs for women than was their initial establishment.

Genesis: Dedicated Leaders With a Mission

The official beginnings of CEW programs span the years 1960–1966, when the climate for their launching was particularly favorable. National concern about the underutilization of talented women, and publicity about foundation financing of the earliest programs stimulated institutional staff members, especially mature women, to voice concerns about the special needs of their gender and age for counseling, convenient scheduling, and new or revised course and program content. Though the initiating forces and their strength varied considerably across institutions, the time was auspicious to provoke an institutional response to this population usually not in the mainstream of higher education.

Leadership, however, was the key. Echoing an observation of Esther Raushenbush, one program director interviewed in our case study stated: "I think something like this has to be a mission on the part of one person in order to get it established, wherever that person happens to be." In all fourteen institutions studied, one or two persons spearheaded the drive for the twin prerequisites of special programs: financial underpinnings and administrative authority.

The latter often proved easier to secure. Some programs were initiated by administrators, in one instance out of admitted pragmatic inclinations: "I knew money was available and sensed it was a 'coming field.' " Three case studies underscore the foresight of presidents or deans who viewed service to special audiences of women as a logical expression of the objectives of their institutions. One urban university president, sensitive to his institution's relationship with minorities, made a speech early in the 1960s committing the institution to create offices that would serve both racial minorities and women. Another president launched a program designed to enable high-achieving women to continue their professional endeavors in the context of a college devoted to academic excellence. One administrator used the institution's history of curricular individualization and flexibility to incorporate special courses and procedures for adult women who wished to complete the baccalaureate. Often initial leadership came from women whose community volunteer efforts had inspired and sharpened their organizational abilities. One CEW program, for example, owes its origins to the combined talents of several civic volunteers who convinced appropriate college officials to offer special programming for adult women.

Early funding of the programs usually came from institutional contributions, especially in the form of space, some equipment and facilities, and modest amounts for clerical and staff salaries. In two institutions, presidents used their discretionary funds to get a program started. One program began and continues to operate on the fees it generates; another, initiated with volunteers, later received a $150,000 grant of federal funds under Title I of the 1965 Higher Education Act. Private foundations and donors, principally the former, contributed to the establishment of some programs or to specially designed projects related to continuing education for women. In a five-year period for example, the Carnegie Corporation provided over $.5 million, ranging from $30,000 to $182,000, for five programs in the case-study sample; the Rockefeller Brothers Fund supported another group with a $250,000 grant; and a small local foundation donated $10,000 to begin a program in its own urban setting.

Once programs were initiated, most institutions delegated planning responsibility to small committees. Eight programs reported that original planning rested with administrative committees, usually composed of two or three staff persons; four other programs indicated that both faculty and administrators were involved. In one college, community representatives were included in a faculty-administrative group; in another, community women accomplished all the initial planning on a volunteer basis. Only two institutions reported using outside consultants.

Initial planning focused on writing proposals for funding or for institutional approval, although the latter rarely involved the usual committee structure and review procedures so integral to most colleges. In fact, administrative assent was granted immediately in a few instances, and a program was established almost instantaneously, especially when the original impetus came from a president or dean. The logistics of most CEW endeavors rested with small administrative committees which instigated the first program offerings—sometimes after studying the needs of a particular population such as alumnae, more often by simply setting up an office and mirroring the services of the earliest program models. Community contact through speeches, media appearances, and discussions with women's organizations added information to the planning process and alerted potential clients to the program's existence. Using volunteer help, one program set up an office to run workshops and discussions on the interests and needs of various groups of women in their community. Another began offering one or two noncredit courses in self-assessment as the initial program thrust and, in the process, gathered information about their clientele. But, however imbued with the spirit of their undertaking, these originators were polite in their tactics and moderate in their requests for institutional support. As one program director emphasized, she showed no intent to inflate her undertaking and was facilitated by her "modest ambition."

The original objectives of the programs were less modest. They reflected a gamut of national and local concerns and individual client needs. The following statements demonstrate a breadth of vision and a general sensitivity to the special needs of mature women:

- to offer an opportunity for alumnae to return for degree completion
- to help young women foresee and plan for a future with "interrupted multiple roles"
- to identify and meet special needs of women in the community
- to facilitate women's reentry into school or work
- to enable talented women to pursue advanced professional study and activity
- to develop special programs where women can be trained quickly and enter the labor market most expeditiously
- to provide services for self-assessment and for both short- and long-range life planning
- to establish a central agency or service for women needing counseling or information
- to offer an opportunity for intellectual reawakening or enrichment.

Each program set goals that touched the breadth of purpose implied in the statements, varying only in emphasis within the special institutional or community context. The original objectives of some were admittedly vague because of uncertainties about the specific needs of their clientele. The flavor or special focus of these first efforts varied from program to program.

As the programs moved from planning to operation, the originators saw themselves as agents accomplishing "societal and individual good," as one interviewee expressed it. The services they offered initially, and their complementary staff and program organization, confirm their highly generalized mission. Eventually they would narrow their focus and at the same time expand their activities as they tried to find an institutional niche and an organizational rationale.

The Programs: Client-Centered Service

If continuing education for women seems ambiguous to the observer, it is not because its goals are not common or clear: The fifteen programs in this study, and others like them across the country, intend to articulate and serve the needs of adult women. They elude definitive description, however, because both their clients and their parent institutions differ, and they respond to these differences with considerable variation in program and resources.

For example, since the beginning of each case-study program, counseling has been a major service. But what it represents as a program component ranges from an office with only a director who sees hundreds of women in a year, typically for one visit, to a service with the equivalent of nine full-time counselors or assistants who provide long-term individual or group counseling including testing, educational and vocational information, self-assessment inventories, and academic advising.

Special services—such as child care, job placement, research projects, or specially focused degree programs—have been available in some continuing education offices from the beginning, but they are certainly not common to all programs even today. And the extent to which programs offer courses, credit or noncredit, varies enormously from those offered on a one-time basis for no credit to those closely integrated with regular college degree programs.

CEW Programs A, B, and C below, all located in the same geographic area, illustrate how programs in this study and elsewhere differ in services, institutional character, populations involved, and available resources.

Program A, a division of a small college for women, is closely integrated with all the activities and objectives of the institution. Originally focused on alumnae who wished to complete undergraduate degrees, the program no longer makes that goal a prerequisite for admission. A small office for Continuing Education offers thorough preadmission counseling and testing, on-going counseling and academic planning, and special once-a-week four-hour seminars "specially designed to reintroduce the student to academic life, capitalize on her maturity and make the most efficient use of her time." Recent seminars included Buddhism, Existentialism and Contemporary Ethics, and Seminar in Contemporary Issues, described as "a detailed study of a central topic. Each year's topic will evolve from new developments in the field of psychology and from the interests of participants."

The program also provides an information bulletin that alerts returning women to such matters as registration or bookstore procedures, calls attention to "regular" classes meeting more conveniently late in the day or on Saturdays, and encourages women to apply for credit-by-examination or "life experience credit." Through counseling, special seminars, and information, the program facilitates a woman's entry into the regular college program, serving as a temporary way-station to reorient her to academic life. The program reaches out to recruit mature women through businesses, hospitals, and community coffee hours. Recently the program has launched business-directed Career Potential Workshops that help a particular firm to encourage new and realistic career goals for women employees. In essence, Program A emphasizes individual assessment and counseling, recruits community women for its offerings, provides a limited but specially designed series of courses to enhance entry into the regular college program, and acts as an intermediary in opening up opportunities within the college for gaining credit for independent study or experience.

In contrast, *Program B* has a less direct relationship to the academic mainstream of its institution, a moderately large land-grant university. This program derives its character from its organizational roots in continuing education and extension, long identified as having a special sensitivity to adults in the "town" rather than "gown" community. Its services focus heavily on the role of women in community cooperation and improvement or on their own assessment and development. Most often program efforts result in short noncredit workshops, lectures, and forums addressed specifically to needs for skill training, or to the special interests of women who either are not enrolled in university degree programs or may be considering later matriculation. For example, Program B offers noncredit courses in women's studies such as Women: A Historical Perspective, The Single Woman in a Couple's Society, and Growing Up Female. One special workshop series encouraged working women to develop appropriate expertise for promotion: Executive Challenge: The Woman Administrator; The Woman Supervisor; and The Woman Manager. Sessions range in length and cost. Conversation Skills for Women involved three sessions for fifteen dollars; Why not College?, a course in study techniques applied to academic disciplines, ran eight weeks for a fee of forty dollars.

Single or multisession workshops frequently emphasize individual self-assessment and redirection, such as Evenings for Becoming, described as "a series of educational encounters designed to sensitize women to the social and cultural effects of the women's movement," and Personal Growth for Women, which was an eight-session series featuring "intense self-exploration, Transactional Analysis and Assertive Training."

A few of this program's commitments are to special funded projects. For example, Lunch and Learn, a series for women employed in local government agencies, is designed to motivate people to job advancement, continuing education, and community involvement; Parent Participation joins together Junior League members and inner-city mothers in a program to train effective community leaders.

Finally, the program provides a Women's Resource Service, "a place where women might come to explore alternatives and choices in their life style." Utilizing a corps of trained volunteers, the Service includes a library of occupational and educational resource materials, promotes programs to sensitize employers to varying dimensions of the women's movement, and accumulates data on clients to improve program services and referrals. Program B, then, includes a wide range of programmatic efforts heavily dependent upon community support and a small staff's ability to assess current needs and interests. Some women enter the regular channels of the university, often as a result of this program's encouragement or referral. The program itself, however, finds its mission in the commitments of the land-grant tradition.

Originally, *Program C* proposed to facilitate the return of women to degree programs in a large research-oriented university with considerable national visibility. Initial offerings included counseling, a major conference on opportunities for women through education, and the continuous individual negotiations necessary to loosen rigid university restrictions in admissions and financial aid—all barriers to mature women hoping to return to their education, often on a part-time basis and with credits acquired many years before.

Program C remains heavily focused on counseling, with a professional staff expanded to meet continuous needs for educational and vocational information, referral services both within the university and to other institutions, and financial and academic advising. Small professionally led groups allow for discussions of single issues common to many women students. A library provides up-to-date resource materials on educational and occupational opportunities and research on women's lives.

But with some university rigidities loosened over the years, often due to its own advocacy role, the program has generated new components to aid a rapidly growing and changing clientele. The number of women seeking counseling has increased tenfold in ten years; in 1970 the largest group seeking services were women under twenty-five. A lecture series brings prominent women scholars to the campus to give major papers. Annual conferences have drawn large audiences for such day-long discussions as New Careers in Community Services, Women in School and at Work, and New Patterns of Employment. Proceedings have been edited and published, reaching programs and individuals throughout the country. Recent conferences emphasize the program's role in promoting research on women's education and development, and scholarship in women's studies. Scholars and graduate students within the university have delivered a series of research summaries and analyses to nationally representative groups, and those papers have become available as part of the program's publications. A scholarship fund solicited by the program from individual donors enables women to complete interrupted education. In cooperation with academic departments, the program also sponsors evening credit courses for women who work or have job responsibilities, and a few noncredit courses specifically to update study techniques.

These synopses illustrate what the case-study programs do to counsel, advise, facilitate, challenge, support, and change women who seek their help and service. The programs have not altered greatly themselves; objectives remain constant, though approaches to meeting these objectives have expanded and become more focused. Staff members, some with over a decade of experience, have grown more certain about what clients need and want. Career programs, job skill training, and orientation to the world of work are now more dominant because, as one chancellor observed, women are more directed toward a career than toward "the good life as wife and mother."

Similarly, the women now in continuing education programs seem more serious about academic work than were their predecessors in the early 1960s; they will not settle for courses with only "dilettante appeal." Their interest in assertiveness training appears related both to their career orientation and to the influence of the women's movement. Several programs reported special sessions for "strengthening women's backbone" and developing their potential for job advancement.

Besides responding to more specific and emerging needs of their clients, programs are at least attempting to serve a more broadly based population. For example, "lunch and learn" programs, carried out in cooperation with state and federal agencies, tend to focus services on working women, often urban, racially mixed, and widely diverse in age. In addition, programs increasingly attend to the special requirements of divorced, single, and widowed women. These attempts to broaden target audiences spring both from the increased sensitivity of staff members and from the pervasive "middle-class guilt" which has hung over these programs since their genesis. Other changes in the programs have come about as the parent institutions grow more flexible with respect to admissions and to the scheduling of part-time students—a flexibility in part attributable to the influence of CEW programs. Staff time and energy once spent "negotiating the system" for women clients may now be directed toward assessing program components and populations, and returning to some earlier objectives as yet unfulfilled: work with undergraduate women for life planning, and attention to research and evaluation.

In summary, after a decade of activity these fifteen programs continue to be client-centered services, as heavily committed to counseling as they were in the beginning but now more focused on career development and credential programs and more deliberate in trying to serve a broader clientele. While variations in institutions and geography produce shadings or extensions of service components, as a whole continuing education for women fits well Samuel Gould's description of nontraditional study: "Most of us agreed that non-traditional is more an attitude than a system and thus can never be defined except tangentially." [Commission on Non-Traditional Study, 1973.]

Organization: Autonomy on a Long Leash

As units of a college or university, how do the continuing education programs for women operate? Who staffs them? Who controls them? How are decisions made? What resources do they have?

Interviews with staff members and administrators in the parent institutions suggest that the fifteen programs enjoy a high degree of autonomy in relation to their major emphases: counseling, special programs, and noncredit courses geared to adult women. They operate informally, perhaps more spontaneous and creative than systematic, and although final decisions most often rest with a program director, she invites and encourages input from other staff members, administrative colleagues, and in a few instances, adult women students. About half the programs use some form of advisory committee to provide ideas, reactions, and general planning directions. The role and composition of such a group varies from institution to institution. For example, in one university the deans act in an advisory capacity, meet twice a year, and respond to informal reports by the program's director or staff. Essentially they provide a sounding board and, in the director's view, "protection" within a large bureaucratic institution. Another program assembles different groups for advice on particular projects. In no instance, however, do such advisory committees wield final policy approval. Some programs simply do not have the time and staff to work with outside advisors, even when it might benefit them.

In general, where noncredit women's activities are concerned, there is little intervention from or even contact with administrators in the parent institution, who technically assume final responsibility for a program. Budget decisions, on the other hand, almost always involve central administrators plus formal procedures and reviews consonant with other departments or programs. And when matters touch the heart of the institution—credit offerings—the decision process includes consultation, negotiation, and final approval by appropriate departments. In such discussions the continuing education program director, usually through formal college channels, seeks departmental assent for particular course offerings and for the assignment of faculty.

The size of the staffs in the fifteen case-study programs varies considerably, ranging from two persons to the equivalent of nineteen. Nine programs had an approximate full-time equivalent of between one and five employees, professional and nonprofessional; one program employed six staff members; and four programs had from eleven to nineteen people. A few programs used volunteers, some of them from other institutional training programs, such as counseling or social work. Although the four largest staffs were in programs affiliated with large universities, size of institution is not necessarily correlated with staff complement. One program at a large urban university functioned with one director and two clerical assistants.

Although two programs started with male directors, most tend to be staffed by women—sometimes women who began as clients and, through the program, acquired appropriate training or experience. Volunteer activities—in religious organizations, the Junior League, the League of Women Voters, and so forth—often figure strongly in the backgrounds of counselors, administrators, and program coordinators. Not infrequently, they are faculty wives who know the institution and enter negotiations with departments as old friends. Sometimes that is an advantage. It can also reinforce the tendency to make requests modest—more polite than insistent in approach.

Teaching faculty come from both inside and outside the institution for noncredit courses and are chosen by the program staff, frequently with advice and recommendations from departments. In a few cases, credit courses are taught only by regular college instructors; but from wherever they are recruited, all faculty need final departmental approval when credit is involved. In two programs, deans or departments assign faculty on their own, though often after informal communication with the director. Pay arrangements vary considerably: Five institutions paid CEW faculty according to regular pay scales or formulae; two institutions negotiated salaries based on the assignment; two paid regular faculty on the institutional scale and outsiders according to special arrangements; and four institutions reported the program faculty were paid at a lower rate than were institutional personnel.

Most programs offered no special training for their teachers, and only in-service training for staff members. Half scheduled one or two orientation sessions to discuss program objectives and the characteristics and expectations of their clientele. Several directors mentioned that they made a practice of talking with individual faculty members about course objectives and the teaching of adult students.

Academic or professional competence and expertise are the primary criteria for choosing staff and faculty. In the interviews, directors placed heavy emphasis on rigorous teaching from articulate, stimulating people, both male and female. One stressed, "We seek the most open-minded, mature-in-thought, if not in years, faculty we can get"; another emphasized, "We don't want anyone talking down to our students." Those responsible for staffing services or courses also insist upon people with understanding and sympathy for the special needs of adult women: "someone who can mix scholarship with a certain amount of kindness and gentleness." Finally, directors hope to find people interested in the program, enthusiastic about its objectives, and flexible enough to be available at the best times for the women enrolled. The overwhelming commitment is to provide quality to their students, who obviously demand it. Minimal turnover in both teaching and nonteaching staffs suggests that the programs are successful in meeting such demands. Faculty in particular tend to attach themselves to a program after their initial teaching experience, primarily because of the quality and enthusiasm of their students.

While perhaps rich in the quality of their personnel, these programs operate with limited finances and physical facilities. Most depend upon general institutional funds or specific allocations from a dean's or vice-president's budget. Six programs in the study must "pay their own way" through tuition and fees—long a requirement in extension and adult education. In contrast to the large sums initially donated by major foundations, grants contribute little to program budgets. What few grants there are come from federal or state treasuries or private donors and usually sustain only special projects of limited duration. Expenditures go for little more than the minimal office and staff maintenence associated with program functions. Volunteers sometimes offer clerical or library or even professional counseling service on a limited time basis. In two programs, budgets are so closely integrated with another department or school that the programs have almost no control over their expenditures.

All fifteen programs have at least some facilities to call their own, though as the site visits showed, space is usually limited to offices and a few conference areas. Rarely do programs have their own building or libraries or lounge areas, and no program reported a child-care center although some had access to facilities operated by other departments. Most programs depend upon the availability of space within the parent institution or in community facilities such as churches, synagogues, and schools. Several directors viewed that dependence as a deterrent to the adult woman client's having more continuous contact with the staff and with her peers.

Within their own carefully prescribed limits of service to women with special needs, the continuing education programs constitute an enclave that is focused but informal in operation, staffed by dedicated, competent, concerned persons, and seemingly free to go about their business, as long as that business does not extend beyond financial and physical limitations or tread on the territory of the academics in the college or university. Do those kinds of organizational ground rules suggest toleration, amusement, or resignation on the part of the larger institution? And how, in fact, are these programs accommodated within the parent organization?

Relation to Parent Institution: on the Fringe

Zealous leadership, humanistic service, democratic operations hardly characterize American higher education in the 1970s. It is difficult to imagine that continuing education for women, whose programs are marked by those very attributes, finds widespread acceptance in the halls of ivy. In truth it does not.

On the surface one might think otherwise. The fifteen programs in the study have formed ties with the larger institution. Seven of them fall under the aegis of Extension, Continuing Education, or General Studies, designations which signify special attention to an adult clientele. The remaining programs find a base in central administrative units such as Academic Affairs, Student Services, or Community Relations. Most program directors report to a dean, associate dean, or director, especially in institutions with large complex structures and specific components which embrace the clientele and objectives of the women's programs; a few report to a vice-president or provost because historically those offices have a special commitment to the programs. In two cases—both small colleges with institutional commitments to adult women's education—the president acts as the final authority.

Administrators interviewed in the study acknowledged the high degree of autonomy which the programs have and saw no reason to curb it. As one official stated, "the program has a simple straightforward mission which is easily understood and supported." A few administrators stressed a need for better connections with other offices in the institution, such as newly established women's studies or affirmative action. They described their own role as supportive, responsible for final fiscal and long-range policy approval, but detached from day-to-day operations and planning. While they considered themselves accessible, their contact with the programs was limited, informal, and unpredictable.

Interaction with other aspects and offices of the parent institutions was equally varied, informal, and ad hoc. It focused mostly on individual student problems, and thus involved student services such as admissions, registration, financial aid, counseling, and health, or on specific program offerings, like credit-bearing courses, and thus involved deans, department chairpersons, or faculty.

In the interviews, administrators assessed the commitment of other administrators, faculty members, and students to continuing education programs for women. Whatever their own pledge, they qualified general institutional favor with specific realities. Other administrators, such as deans and vice presidents, they judged to be supportive (1) if they were aware of the programs, and (2) after priorities in the "regular" academic program or research efforts of the university had been met. In contrast to such qualified support, the representatives of three small colleges with programs linked closely to institutional objectives considered commitment "absolute." One dean, however, followed that estimate with, "it's the finest fringe activity the college has."

Comments on faculty and student attitudes toward these programs linked positive support to direct involvement. Administrators based their perceptions on the limited but mostly favorable feedback they received. In some cases they found a kind of "missionary zeal" on the part of faculty who wished to be involved with program activities or classes. Other administrators called attention to positive faculty attitudes as a result of the students themselves. One college official commented that "in the last five years with high school standards relaxed, it's a joy to teach continuing education." But, in the view of administrators, faculty members uninvolved in program teaching or planning tended to ignore any institutional efforts not a part of their daily lives. Once in a while the program enjoyed visibility because of a program director's efforts. "She makes converts," one officer admitted. The general response, however, followed this line: "It's not a program close enough to the mainstream to expect much feedback."

Students appeared even less aware of continuing education for women than faculty. Contact, limited to a few shared classes, touches relatively few "regular" undergraduates. Most, "doing their own thing," are no more nor less aware of this program on their campus than of any other department or activity with which they have no contact. On the other hand, those regular undergraduates who do share classes with adults were judged to be supportive of the ideas that stimulated special programs.

The truth is, then, that programs of continuing education for women have a few "friends in court," mostly administrators who either shepherded their establishment or find their efforts understandable and unobtrusive. A handful of faculty supporters appreciated the competence and rich backgrounds of mature adult students. Students, other than the adults themselves, have long been oblivious to anything but their immediate concerns.

No, if generalizations can be drawn from a group of sample cases, these programs do not enjoy widespread acceptance in the parent institutions though the attitude is one of indifference rather than rejection. The majority of people in the academic community do not even know they are there. Their values—client-centered, service-oriented, informal, even organizationally irrational—are antithetical to traditional academic selectivity and rationality. While one might conclude that their independence reflects their virtues, in fact it is more likely a statement of institutional indifference. When all is said and done, they depend heavily for their existence on their own propriety and on the largess of some administrator. With few exceptions they are on the periphery of academic decisionmaking and very much outside the traditional reward system: scholarship, not service. In only those few small colleges which centrally embrace the same goals do the programs for mature women have visible significance, though even in those cases their activities are so intertwined with those of the institution that it is difficult to distinguish them.

Institutions are no more overtly hostile to those programs than the programs are to them. But if continuing education programs for women are to be maintained or expanded, the successes they claim, the problems they face, and the priorities of their financially beleaguered institutions must be closely scrutinized.

Self-Assessment: Expansion Versus Fiscal Reality

Limited budgets and staffs substantially curtail formal, systematic evaluation by the programs themselves. Most assessment consists of informal feedback from students, staff members, or teachers; some follow-up data on the educational and employment situations of previous clients; and occasionally special summary reports or dissertations. A few programs follow regular institutional procedures, including budget reviews and student evaluations. Activities which depend upon fees or tuition measure their success simply by enrollments. In the fifteen programs, only a few research efforts had focused on the academic achievement of clients, on their career aspirations, or on their social and psychological development as a result of program services. In the absence of outside advisory bodies, or of continuous administrative examination, directors and their staffs carry the burden of judgment about their own strengths and weaknesses. For most, assessment proves difficult, frustrating, and admittedly subjective.

Program directors and administrators in the larger institutions were asked to identify successes, problems, and possible improvements in their programs. As Table 2-1 indicates, they were relatively consistent in singling out successful activities. Counseling, for example, drew strong praise for fulfilling the commitment to the individual woman. As a "haven for women interested in continuing education," these services carved out a role in changing women's attitudes about themselves, in convincing them that "they're not deadwood." Other positive comments by program directors reflect this positive assessment and suggest, as well, the varied interpretations of the counseling function as (1) being a successful method for reaching individual women, and (2) being a central place for women to get help, and (3) consistently providing heavy feedback—it has made real and positive differences in women's lives. Course offerings, both credit and noncredit, were also identified as successes, with particular emphasis given to the academic talent of the women themselves. One director observed that courses fostered "a new respect that faculty and adults from the community have gained for each other."

Program directors noted the success of special projects with focused audiences, such as career-oriented training projects or "certificate programs which provide a new level of competency and self-sufficiency." Administrators emphasized the quality of the program themselves; a dean, for example, declared, "She [the program director] hasn't stooped to frivolous handicraft." They also mentioned public relations value in the community, an assessment which befits administrators who must frequently play the role of spokespersons and representatives of the institution at large. "We are educational brokers reaching out to the community," one administrator suggested. Another commented that continuing education programs had attracted women in the community who became supportive of the university for the excellence they found in program offerings.

While program directors and administrators spoke with assurance about the success of the programs in meeting the needs of adult women and in contributing to improved community relations, their sense of overall impact, inside and outside the institution, seemed less clear. After initial responses ranging from "tremendous" and "enormous" to "zero-to-date" and "marginal and intangible," program directors identified three fairly discrete ways in which their efforts seemed to have impact: (1) awareness, (2) advocacy, and (3) local and national leadership. Several directors emphasized that awareness and appreciation for adults as students stemmed from the initial presence of returning women. "Colleges had no idea adults were as able, intelligent, and as motivated as the people who have come to them through this port of entry," one continuing education leader stressed. Another commented pointedly that the impact had accumulated over the years and represented "some toning down of the arrogance of the young." With respect to advocacy, faculty votes to change rigid admissions, scheduling, and credit policies—often solicited by the program's personnel—opened institutions to diverse age and occupational groups as well as to minorities such as women. Some felt the presence of the programs on campus facilitated other efforts for women: women's studies, research projects, and special counseling resources. As one program director remarked: "the program provides leadership on and off campus in terms of trying to do something for and about women." Administrators reinforced that observation and often expressed appreciation for the program's role in acting as an "ameliorating, stabilizing force," which made women's studies easier to understand and accept, and which fostered openness to the needs of nontraditional students for flexible administrative policies. One institution considered its program as the catalyst for a statewide credit-by-examination policy and also judged that it had "indirectly affected the development of a new degree in nontraditional study." Another administrator ventured a bit tentatively: "I hope it's contributed to flexible administration—people in the university often fear bending roles."

In the main, however, directors sensed that their contributions were made more often outside their campus. For them, their major impact lies in their influence on women and organizations in the community, in consultation with emerging programs at other institutions, in public appearances, and in leadership in national adult education. One director summed up the situation of many when she assessed her program's impact as "very, very great on women everywhere across the country," but emphasized that her own institution "thinks these women are dilettantes; they don't take them seriously." Finally, a program director in another university concluded that her efforts had not favorably altered the program's budget or enabled a single woman to occupy a top administrative job. Her program had, she believed, "made the administration *aware* but not *imperative* regarding women."

Institutional administrators made global evaluations from, "it hasn't caused major upheaval" to "it permeates everything we do," or "the program staff are wonderful ambassadors demonstrating a certain human approach to education." Beyond a generally favorable sense of the continuing education programs for women, administrators could offer few specifics. "It's hard to trace," one admitted, "the whole educational world has shifted regarding nontraditional study." One president, however, cited diminishing regular student populations and considered this program simply as "a lifesaver for money."

Reports on the impediments to the program—their major problems or obstacles—center on finances and the question of expansion. Program directors viewed as their major problems a need for expanded staff, program, and facilities to handle larger and more varied audiences. Some programs now attract women more diverse in academic background, age, economic circumstance, and career orientation, but they cannot deliver appropriate counseling, child care, courses, or training to meet the needs of these women. Others, cognizant of their middle-class suburban origins and emphasis, lack the financial aid funds, special programming, or facilities that would help them recruit and serve new populations. Program directors frequently linked program problems to precarious financial conditions, including

- dependence upon fees—usually too high for urban and low-income women—to support program activities
- insufficient and unstable budgetary support from general institutional funds
- the absence of financial aid for part-time students, an increasingly significant factor for middle-class suburban as well as low-income women

One director emphasized, "we could double our population if we had financial and scholarship help."

Other obstacles such as being "at the mercy of departments and schools" for offerings, or the need for wider institutional communication and cooperation seemed less painful but no less real. "It is a constant job," one director noted, "to stay legitimate and to educate other areas of the university regarding the flexibility and needs of the nontraditional student." One president acknowledged difficulties between faculties and programs to find appropriate time frames or specially designed courses for women clients. Another administrator saw the program's dilemmas as stemming from the reluctance of "obstinate deans to go the extra mile regarding course sequences" and from having to deal with a bureaucratic system which was not geared to do such things as generate special transcripts. The consensus, however, suggested that dealing with problems or making improvements meant first overcoming dwindling, unpredictable financial resources. "There is no limit to what we could do if we had financial resources," one official in a parent institution commented.

What people involved in the programs would to to improve them is clear: They would move directly to expand past successes and to broaden functions related to a swiftly changing social scene. Specifically they would enlarge counseling staffs with persons trained specifically to counsel adults, and they would increase their attention to career-oriented training, vocational planning, and job placement. "It's unethical to bring back women and hold a job up as a carrot and then not give them a job," one director lamented. With current resources, most programs simply cannot offer placement services. Although reluctant to specify the extent of current demands for services, program directors were particularly pained by their inability to enlarge their clientele to include more minority, working-class, inner-city, and undergraduate women.

Logically, administrators view improvement from a different vantage point. Their concerns focus on adequate financial security and organizational rationality—aspects of institutional stability frequently linked. Reorganization to piece together segments of their campuses serving similar functions or audiences occurred to more than one dean or vice-president. For them, tightening to avoid duplication, to sharpen cooperation and communication, and to instigate systematic planning and evaluation would take precedence over attempts to expand audiences or services.

For the most part, directors and their administrative colleagues generate a favorable image of their continuing education programs for women. They note the success of counseling, courses, and other activities which reach individuals and groups in their locale and elsewhere. Some fruitful policy changes in the institutions at large can be attributed to frequent efforts by program staffs to increase acceptance of nontraditional students. Faculty in contact with such students find them highly motivated and above average academically.

Despite their "good works," the programs face the dilemma of wanting, often needing, to expand operations and widen their outreach but finding that financial restrictions seriously threaten even the status quo. Not only are they peripheral to the institution's major thrust, but also they are not sure how much security they can derive from general institutional funding or administrative protection. Their administrative colleagues, on the other hand, feel that financial stability depends upon more systematic operations and priorities. In fact, some comments from deans and other officials suggest that if these programs were expanded, their own acceptance of them might end. At best they are hesitant to

Table 2–1
Perceived Successes or Strengths of CEW Programs

	Program Directors	Administrators	Total
Counseling	10	8	18
Academic emphasis/faculty support	2	2	4
Courses, credit and noncredit	7	7	14
Special projects, focused on special needs or populations	3	2	5
Advocacy/leadership, campus and community	3	4	7
Public relations, especially community	0	8	8
Self-supporting	0	3	3
Quality of staff and offerings	0	3	3
Success/satisfaction of women	0	6	6
No response	0	3	3

commit themselves. For example, one provost remarked: "It's a relatively inexpensive operation as the director has run it; whether she could contribute more with more staff, I don't know." That this dilemma and other tensions between programs and institutions must be addressed seems inevitable when higher education is confronting grim economic and social realities.

**Part II
Women and Their Families**

3

Adult Development and Education

Helen S. Astin

In the late 1960s and early 1970s, higher education became aware of the presence on its campuses of a more diverse group of students than it had previously served and came to realize the need to develop new goals and programs for these students. This emerging concern is reflected in the recent proliferation of innovative educational approaches, such as external degree programs, flexible curricula and requirements, open universities, and other forms of nontraditional study.

As institutions open their doors and reach out to new and atypical populations—e.g., veterans, housewives, second-careerists—they face the challenge of providing appropriate and flexible curricula. Little information exists, however, about the personal characteristics, modes of learning, or specific needs and interests of these populations—necessary information if such curricula are to be designed. This study was intended to correct part of that deficiency.

In designing the present study and formulating the specific questions to be answered, we drew on three somewhat diverse but overlapping areas of scholarly interest:

1. Studies of adult development: These highlight the developmental interests and concerns of adults and provide a framework that permits us to ground our questions, findings, and interpretations in existing evidence about what adults are like, what their needs are, and what values they hold and express.
2. Studies of the educational needs of adults: These describe what adult education is, who takes advantage of it, and what their purposes and goals are.
3. Studies of the continuing education needs of women and of programs designed to meet these needs.

Adult Development

Scholars in the field of adult development [e.g., Flavell, 1970; Neugarten, 1964, 1973; Simon, 1968] generally agree that, whereas children and adolescents actively assimilate experiences, adults passively accommodate to them. Children's cognitive development is based on their physical

45

development and maturational processes, but the cognitive style of adults is based on unprogrammed experiences, such as marriage, parenting, and work, and on programmed experiences, such as psychotherapy and adult education. While youth is described as a period of searching for identity, adulthood is depicted as a period of searching for "integrity" and avoiding despair [Erickson, 1963]. But theoreticians may fail to recognize that women in adult education are searching not only for integrity but also for identity; they are asking themselves who they are beyond being wives and mothers.

The coping styles of men and women in later life differ. Whereas men become more affiliative as they mature, women show a greater need for independence, become more outgoing and assertive, and remove themselves to some degree from the nurturing role [Brim, 1974; Lowenthal, 1973]. A study by Baruch [1967] of college-educated women indicates that a temporal cycle in the achievement motive is evident, dependent on age and family situation. Thus, a period of high need for achievement before beginning a family is followed by a decline in achievement need. But once the children are grown, there is a return to the previous high level. Given these observed sex differences in the characteristics and behaviors of adults, it is easy to understand the need for redirection and accomplishment and the work orientation that adult women returning to education have. Yet not only are these women redefining themselves in terms of new roles and experiences; they also typify the adult learner. Like all adult learners, they are conscious of their reasons for learning, and they understand the benefits of education [Tough, 1968].

The existing literature has focused on the developmental differences between youth and adulthood and between adult men and adult women. So far, no attempt has been made to differentiate among groups of women on the basis of their past roles and experiences. Most of the literature centers on women whose primary roles have been wife and mother. The similarities and differences between these women and women who have made career commitments have not been examined. One wonders, do career women go through the same adult crises as those observed in the male population? Do they, like men, come to have a greater need for affiliation and nurturance as they grow older?

Similarly, most studies of women in adult education programs have focused on women in search of identity and integrity, women who have new outwardly directed goals, who require more assertive behaviors, and who are actively assimilating new experiences. Only a few studies have included women who have always been career-oriented and who have returned to update their skills or to develop new skills in pursuit of a second career. More information on these women is needed.

In addition to addressing questions central to issues of adult development, this study provides information on the complex interactions between family situation and educational/occupational outcomes. It also makes possible a close look at the socialization processes that result in sex-role expectations and behaviors which in turn affect the educational and occupational development of women. Thus, we were concerned with such questions as: How do internalized sex roles, and support (or lack of it) from important others (spouse, children) affect a woman's self-concept, aspirations, and achievements? The attitudes and behavior on the part of the immediate family elicit what kinds of perceptions and behaviors on the part of women with respect to their sense of personal worth, emotional well-being and mental health, need for achievement, motivation, and accomplishment?

Because of their diversity—in age, in socioeconomic background, in education, in career continuity/discontinuity—adult women in continuing education programs provide a unique opportunity to examine the complexities that exist in the educational and career development of women. Their age range, for example, permits us to analyze the interests, aspirations, and concerns of women from age twenty-five to age sixty-five and over.

Adult Education

Examining the general literature on adult education, one finds four terms—adult education, continuing education, recurrent education, and life-long learning—that are often used interchangeably, though each denotes a slightly different concept. *Adult education* refers to vocational and avocational courses designed specifically for adults and offered by secondary schools and community agencies. *Continuing education* refers to educational programs developed to help adults upgrade their education and their occupational skills and offered in a postsecondary setting. Because it is more common and more easily defined in terms of program offerings, it is the term that is used throughout the book. The terms *recurrent education* and *lifelong learning* are more global, referring not so much to specific and limited programs and courses as to the concept of regular and repeated opportunities, throughout the individual's lifetime, to return to education (either to train for new skills and better jobs or to learn for learning's sake). *Recurrent education* is primarily the European term and *lifelong learning* is its American equivalent.

Recurrent education, a concept pioneered chiefly by the Center for Educational Research and Innovation of the Organization for Economic Cooperation and Development, provides for "new relationships between individuals, educational opportunities, and working careers that would lead to more equity between social classes, ethnic and age groups, men and women" [Gass, 1973]. It implies a redistribution of education, so that it occurs not in one lump at the beginning of a person's life but over the life span, thus permitting for leisure, work, and education at alternating periods. Its premises are:

1. Learning can take place at any time.
2. Learning should be equitable: The goal of recurrent education is to achieve educational and social equality.
3. Continuous learning is necessary because of rapid changes and growth in knowledge in a technological society.
4. Work and social experiences should be important considerations in admissions and in curricular designs.

Since the primary purpose of recurrent education is to reduce inequality and offer a second chance, it is clear that women's stake in recurrent education is closely allied to their concerns for equality of opportunity and equal rights legally, educationally, and vocationally. Moreover, recurrent education provides opportunities for career development and a means of updating skills that have become obsolete because of long-term interruptions for family life. Recurrent education epitomizes the current emphasis on equal educational opportunity that characterizes efforts begun in the 1960s. Prior to that time, a supposedly meritocratic educational policy prevailed in America, though it was biased in favor of merit in men. The wave for a more egalitarian educational policy paralleled the efforts of women leaders to establish continuing education programs for women, even though only recently has a national conference on recurrent education taken place (sponsored by the National Institute of Education in 1973, Washington, D.C. DHEW) and a visible publication appeared [Vermilye, ed., *Lifelong Learners: A New Clientele for Higher Education,* 1974].

Adult women in continuing education programs constitute only one part of the population of adults seeking education, however. In 1962, under sponsorship of the Carnegie Corporation, Johnstone and Rivera undertook a general inquiry into the nature of continuing education in America. They found that approximately 25 million adults—about equally divided between the sexes—were active in some form of learning during the year of the study. About half of them had enrolled part-time in courses and activities ranging from the vocational through the recreational to the academic. The median age of participating adults was 36.5. They were somewhat better educated than the typical adult and were more likely to hold white-collar than blue-collar jobs. Among persons under 35, a substantially higher proportion of men than women were engaged in learning activities. Adults in general were likely to indicate that they were taking courses out of interest and a desire for knowledge rather than for specific occupational objectives, though men were more likely than women to say that their educational activities were related to occupational goals. The more facilities available in a given community, the more likely were the adults in the community to participate in such activities.

The authors of the study concluded, as early as 1962, that the potential clientele for continuing education would increase more rapidly than the population as a whole and that learning-for-work and learning-for-leisure would together come to dominate the adult education scene to an even greater extent in the future than was observed at the time of the survey. Other studies investigating the educational needs of adult women and the programs designed to serve them report similar findings. Today, Johnstone and Rivera's predictions have become a reality and one can now forecast that growth will continue.

Continuing Education Programs for Women

As was detailed in Chapter 1, the first continuing education programs for women emerged in the early 1960s. According to the Women's Bureau of the Department of Labor [1974], in 1963 there were only about twenty such programs; 100 such programs had been identified by 1966, and 376 schools with specific programs for adult women were listed, with a brief program description, in 1971. As was also noted in the first chapter, however, research by Mattfeld [1971] and by Mulligan [1973] indicates that these programs varied considerably in the quality and extent of their services for women. In a survey of the 376 programs, Mulligan received 190 responses, of which 61 indicated that they provided no special services or programs to accommodate the needs of mature women. She surmised that they were included in the Women's Bureau listing either because they offered courses of interest to women or because they offered courses at times convenient to women.

Nevertheless there has been a rapid expansion of continuing education programs for women, and to a large extent, it is the result of the rapid increase in the number of women seeking employment outside the home. As of October 1973, there were 25.5 million women workers twenty-five years of age or over in the United States. Between 1960 and 1973, the number of women in the labor force registered a 39 percent increase, attributable to such factors as technological advances that reduce the demands of housework, declining birth rates, longer life spans, rising costs of living, and the encouragement and support provided to women by the women's movement.

Continuing education programs for women were originally developed to facilitate the entry or reentry into the academic world of women past the traditional age of eighteen. The creation of these programs was prompted, first, by concern over humanpower shortages and the waste of human abilities that the institutionalization of the housewife represented and, second, by a growing awareness that many housewives suffered from dissatisfaction with their lives, which seemed boring and meaningless to them. Sensitive both to the waste of human resources and the plight of the American housewife, many women leaders in academic institutions worked to establish continuing education programs for women. But their efforts were not always appreciated by the institutions that employed them; college and university administrators often balked at such programs, feeling that it did not fall within their purview to facilitate the entry into the academic world of nontraditional students, especially women.

A review of the literature shows that women who decide to continue their education can be divided into two large groups: those whose ultimate goal is a career (or at least employment) and those who want to take some courses or a few seminars out of general interest, perhaps to complete a degree, but who have no intention of seeking employment. Within that first large group, there are several subgroups. Many women must go to work to support or help support themselves and their families, so they come to continuing education programs to gain marketable skills or to update long-unused ones. As technology advances, the casual, semiskilled, or unskilled jobs that have long served as important sources of employment for women are dwindling [London, 1966]; thus, women now need more specialized abilities in order to find jobs. A second subgroup comprises women who have jobs but who have found that, without a college degree, they have no opportunity for advancement. A third subgroup consists of those who have been employed for a number of years and are now preparing for mid-life career changes, either out of dissatisfaction with their current jobs or because rapid changes have made their jobs obsolete. The fourth subgroup, and probably the largest proportion of women in continuing education, consists of those whose family demands have lessened and who now find work a viable and appealing opportunity.

The women who enter programs for reasons other than employment may be motivated by a variety of factors. Perhaps they are simply interested in learning more about the revolutionary advances occurring in so many fields; the rapid proliferation of knowledge has made education a life-long endeavor. They may be drawn by purely avocational interests.

They may find they are bored; their husbands are busy, their children are in school or grown up, and volunteer activities no longer seem satisfying. They may be taking refuge from marital and family problems. Finally, many women who enroll in degree programs do so because they left college to work or get married and only now find themselves in a position to complete the course work toward the degrees they began working for previously.

Whatever their reasons for wanting to reenter the academic world, women who are considering this decision confront a number of problems, both personal and institutional. The first personal problem that a woman faces if she considers returning to school is ignorance of how to go about doing so. One investigator writes: "We found that as women become increasingly aware of the fact that it is possible to resume or begin a career, . . . there is a confusion and a hesitancy about just how they may pick up the reins" [Hunter, 1965, p. 311]. Although she wants to work, a woman may not be sure what vocation would best suit her particular capabilities and interests. She may not even know exactly what her aptitudes and abilities are. The woman who does know what she would like to do may be uncertain about whether she has the necessary qualifications for the job. Could she be a psychologist? What kind of training would she need, how long would it take, and where could she get it? She has a number of questions and no idea of where to find the answers.

Another major personal problem is the lack of confidence in her own capabilities that a woman almost invariably feels after she has been away from school for some length of time, particularly if she has been a homemaker in the interim. She is apprehensive about her ability to take notes, to remember material covered in reading assignments, to use the library properly, and to write papers and exams. Afraid she will not be able to keep up with the eighteen- to twenty-year-olds, she hesitates to enter competitive academic situations. Speaking of continuing education programs, Eleanor Dolan says: "The key to success is the ability to instill confidence in women returning to college. This is the common denominator of every successful program" [Scates, 1966, p. 6].

Some women who are considering a return to school worry about being isolated from the other, younger, students because of the disparity in their ages. These women are afraid that they will be unable to relate to any of their classmates. This fear of being alone and labeled as different is enough to dissuade some from taking the step of enrolling in a college or university.

Guilt is yet another problem with which women returning to school must cope. Because of an internalized concept of their role as self-sacrificing wife and mother, women feel guilty about leaving or, as they see it, "abandoning" their homes and families to undertake a time-consuming venture that they find so personally fulfilling. Are they being selfish, indulging their own whims and spending the family's money—money that could have gone toward a vacation trip or the children's college educations? They may, in fact, feel guilty about aggressively pursuing the education they want; perhaps this aggressiveness will be interpreted by others as an indication that they are trying to compete with their husbands. Various societal attitudes reinforce these guilt feelings. Such attitudes about a woman's place (in the home) and a woman's proper role (supportive, compliant wife, nurturant mother) may lead family and friends to pressure the woman into remaining at home. In such instances, it is hard to brave criticism from those one respects and loves and to find the courage to stick to plans that will alter the family and societal pattern of living.

These, then, are some of the personal problems that women who consider returning to school must deal with before they take even the initial step of enrolling. And, of course, the uncertainties, fears, and guilts may continue and mount once she has taken that step. The women's movement has helped somewhat to alleviate these problems, both by influencing the attitudes of society and by influencing the woman's attitude toward herself, especially her sense of her own personal worth and her sense of her rights as an individual. Thus, some of these problems are not today the major impediments that they were in the early 1960s and before. But they still exist.

Once a woman has managed to overcome her personal problems enough to arrive at the college or university, she encounters institutional roadblocks. Although there is no longer any question about the equal educability of men and women [Crosman and Gustav, 1966], colleges and universities have traditionally been somewhat ambivalent about undertaking the education of women, particularly of "mature" women.

Admissions procedures are the first obstacle. Brandenberg [1974] illuminates the problem clearly when she states that admissions requirements for reentering adults may not be valid since their transcripts and letters of recommendation from past professors and teachers are outdated. High school or college transcripts ten or fifteen years old are not very impressive to an admissions officer, especially if they date from a time when the applicant was more concerned with her social than with her academic life. Whom can a woman returning to school ask for recommendations? It is unlikely that any of her teachers remember her sufficiently well to be able to write an accurate evaluation of her aptitudes and academic promise, both of which may have changed radically in the interim. College entrance tests are designed for high school students recently enrolled in courses whose material is covered in the tests. A woman who has been out of school for fifteen years—or even for five—may find that her algebra skills and her knowledge of American history are inadequate to answer the questions on achievement tests in those fields.

Most colleges and universities will not accept college credits past a certain period. Therefore, a woman who completed her sophomore year twelve years ago finds she must begin all over again. If her credits are within the time limitations but earned at another college, the institution she is applying to now may accept some course credits but refuse others. Each school has its own set of often rather arbitrary rules and regulations about the transfer of credits. Frequently a student does not learn what credits have and have not been transferred until after she is enrolled because, in many cases, each department must rule on whether to accept courses related to its field of study. The discouraging probability of losing some or all previously acquired credits has prevented many women from completing the degrees they began earlier. Moreover, only a few institutions have come to accept that learning goes on outside the classroom. A woman who has spent some years out of the academic world serving as a volunteer in community organizations, raising a family, or working at a job has learned through immediate experience. The difference between the depth and breadth of her experience and that of the average eighteen-year-old student who comes straight from high school is vast. But in most cases, the institution treats them identically, demanding that they fulfill the same course requirements. This situation seems particularly ironic in view of the recent trend toward work-study educational arrangements whereby a student earns college credits for work experience.

Yet another institutional obstacle involves student aid: Such programs are not designed for the thirty-five-year-old student although her need may be as great or greater than that of any other student. Unemployed married women are dependent on their husbands' approval, as Durchholz and O'Connor point out, because in most states if the husband "does not consent to share his income for her tuition or will not sign a student loan application, she will not be able to go to college. She will be ineligible for financial aid because of her husband's earnings" [1973, p. 62]. Traditionally, financial aid has been available only to full-time students. But because of family demands, many women in continuing education programs can enroll in courses only as part-time students. Mulligan writes: "Students who attend school part-time generally do so because they have responsibilities and commitments which preclude full-time attendance. Rather than exhibiting a responsiveness, however, to the high degree of motivation and great need associated with such attendance, the Federal Government has concentrated its program of financial assistance on full-time students" [1973, p. 14]. This has been a very real barrier to the many women who must put the family's needs ahead of the luxury of an education.

That institutions of higher education tend to frown on part-time students, except in night school, raises other problems for the returning woman. For instance, many returning students are trying to prepare themselves academically so that they will be ready to enter the labor force when their children are older. But because of their current family obligations, they must enroll as part-time students. What these women need are classes scheduled during the day, when their children are in school, or if they have preschoolers, classes scheduled at a time—nights or weekends—when another adult is available to babysit. The working woman, of course, requires a different set of scheduling options. Other women want to qualify as rapidly as possible for employment; their need is for accelerated programs. Since the returning adult woman does not live on campus and has many other responsibilities in addition to schoolwork, classes that meet four or five days a week for one hour are usually much less convenient than longer sessions once or twice weekly, or independent study. In short, if the needs of women continuing their education are to be met, a variety of programs and of scheduling options must be made available.

University regulations and policies often make for additional complications. Residence requirements are especially troublesome. In our highly mobile society a married woman working toward a degree is likely to be faced with a move during the college years. If she enters a new college in her final year of study, she may be confronted with an institutional regulation that students spend two years in residence in order to receive the degree. Rigid requirements about courses and class prerequisites meant to guide the younger student may be a source of irritation to returning students. Physical education requirements have come most frequently under attack. Busy adult women find it difficult enough to fit academic classes into their full schedules without the addition of gym courses.

All these problems and complications add up, making the return to higher education a formidable undertaking for a woman who has been away from the academic world for a while. As Brandenberg points out, "The uncertainty and insecurity of [older women students] may be exacerbated by college services that are geared for younger students in a different life situation" [1974, p. 15]. Before the advent of continuing education programs for women, adult women who did manage to enroll in degree programs through official channels had to be highly motivated and not easily daunted, fitting their lives into the pattern dictated by the unyielding and usually unsympathetic institution.

Continuing education programs for women were established by people who recognized that these problems were major impediments to women contemplating a return to school or work. These leaders developed programs to help women make the transition with as few extraneous complications as possible. They very existence of these programs provides a psychological boost to the woman considering venturing out from the household. They are proof that she is not alone, that she will be meeting and attending classes with women in a similar position who share some of her problems and concerns. They attest to the possibility that, as an adult woman, she can go to college or begin a career; others like her have done it successfully. The programs also give evidence of the institution's willingness to help adult women and that it believes in their worth as students.

Counseling is the first aspect of continuing education that most women encounter. Through individual or group counseling they learn to assess themselves more realistically in an atmosphere supportive of self-exploration. In the counseling setting, the emphasis is usually on becoming aware of one's strong points, one's capabilities, values, and aptitudes. Testing is often a part of this self-evaluation process. Information and guidance about appropriate existing programs and vocational information is available. For instance, if a woman wants to become a legal assistant, the counseling service can tell her—or show her how to find—what institutions offer this specialty and what the programs are like. Group counseling often makes extensive use of guest speakers. For instance, women who have returned to work, combining career and family, may be invited to share their experiences and feelings with the group. Employers in the area speak on manpower needs, job opportunities, and job requirements. Representatives from the college or university come to discuss academic requirements, courses, the demand for graduates, and the academic success of mature students. Such skills as how to write a job resume or handle a job interview are often taught. Support from counselors and from other women in the group is an essential aspect of the counseling situation for most women. This support provides the reassurance and social approval they need in order to act. Through the counseling experience—and the self-analysis it encourages—women learn more about themselves and about the realities of the current academic and work worlds they are considering entering. Armed with this information, they are in a much stronger position to make a decision and to implement it.

If, subsequent to counseling or on her own initiative, a woman decides to take courses at a college or university, the continuing education program often has additional services to offer her. Some programs make available credit and noncredit classes, tailored to meet the needs and interests of the returning student and covering a wide spectrum of subjects. Both skill-oriented courses and liberal arts curricula are usually offered. Frequently, classes are scheduled at locations—churches and community buildings—throughout the city and its suburbs, making them more accessible. To attend one of these classes, a woman pays the course fee to the continuing education program itself. She does not have to apply to the university to be accepted and, except for rare occasions, a high school or college diploma is not required; prerequisites are minimal.

Some continuing education programs offer refresher courses, tutorial assistance, or orientation sessions to women contemplating a return to school. These services permit them to brush up on skills that they have not used for some time (e.g., working math problems, writing papers, taking notes). They give women a chance to familiarize themselves with the college setting and to regain confidence in their ability to handle academic work.

At some institutions college degrees are offered through continuing education programs, located in the Extension Division or the College of General Studies, while other programs act as intermediaries, enrolling degree applicants at the parent institution. Some serve more as a clearinghouse, informing women of existing programs which fit their needs.

Certification programs are a unique service offered by some continuing education programs for women. Requiring a year or less of class work, these certificate courses prepare women for jobs that demand specialized skills: e.g., legal assistant, counseling assistant, landscape architect assistant. Women who want to test out their interest in a field or who are reluctant to undertake years of academic course work in preparing for a career can acquire skills that enable them to work in their chosen area of interest within a year's time. Such programs are of special value to divorced or widowed women without job skills who are faced with the necessity of supporting themselves and their children for the first time, allowing them to qualify relatively rapidly for jobs requiring some specialized skills.

Each continuing education program differs from the next, but the basic goal of facilitating and aiding in the back-to-school transition is common to all. Counseling is offered to help each woman in her search for direction and to supply her with information about available options. The program serves as an intermediary with the parent institution, assisting women in handling rigid academic regulations or in bypassing them through admittance to the institution via the continuing education program. Conditional admission, credit for life experience, part-time study, convenient class scheduling in terms of location, time, and frequency of meetings, and the relaxation of class prerequisites—all are essential elements of continuing education programs designed to serve the needs of adult women returning to institutions of higher education.

4

A Profile of the Women in Continuing Education

Helen S. Astin

Who are the women who participate in continuing education programs? The survey questionnaire used in this study was designed to obtain information on a number of areas that describe populations and identify their special needs, current areas of interest and involvement, educational and occupational aspirations, as well as their perceptions of self in relation to family members, relatives and friends, and other women. More specifically, we focused on the following questions:

- What are the demographic and background characteristics and educational and occupational status of these women?
- What are their educational and occupational aspirations?
- What are their reasons for returning to education?
- What are their goals?
- What are the catalytic factors that prompted their return?
- What obstacles have they faced?
- How have the women changed as a result of the program?
- How has the women's movement affected them?
- What do they perceive to be the reactions of their husbands and children?
- What views do they hold of the program itself?

In addition to women who, at the time of the survey, were involved in continuing education programs (referred to as *participants; N* = 649), we were also interested in women who had participated in such a program three to five years earlier but were not currently involved in CEW (referred to as *alumnae; N* = 541). We sought answers to the following questions:

1. How do the two groups compare?
2. Have there been changes over time in the demographic and background characteristics of women in continuing education programs?
3. What are the alumnae doing now? How many and what kinds of educational activities are they engaged in? Are they employed, and if so, in what occupational areas?

To give perspective to the findings about these two groups of women who either were or had been involved in continuing education, the discussion that follows also makes reference to another group who are in many ways comparable: women over age thirty-one in the general college population. For convenience these women will be termed *adult college women*. We will also mention occasionally comparable figures for women of all ages in the general college population.[1]

This chapter is divided into five sections. The first profiles the demographic characteristics of women in continuing education. The second discusses their educational status and aspirations. In the third, their occupational status and plans are considered. The fourth section covers a variety of more personal material, including their self-ratings and attitudes, and their relations with their husbands and children. The final section deals in greater detail with the experiences of these women in relation to continuing education, including their objectives, the obstacles they encountered, and their recommendations for improving the programs.

Demographic Characteristics

The median age of the participants was thirty-six, with a range from eighteen to seventy-five years of age. The alumnae tended to be slightly older, with a median age of forty and a range from nineteen to seventy years of age. Slightly less than one-third of both groups were in the age thirty-one to forty category. Three in ten of the participants but only one-fifth of the alumnae were thirty or under, whereas half of the alumnae but only 37 percent of the participants were over forty.[a] The age differences between the two groups are explained in part by our selection of the two samples to represent different time cohorts; they may also indicate, however, that younger women are becoming more interested in continuing education.

Both groups were predominantly white (94 percent of the participants, 95 percent of the alumnae). Only 3 percent in each group were black, the remainder being Asian American, American Indian, or Spanish-speaking. This preponderance of whites may seem surprising when one considers that, among adult college women, only 63 percent were white, 26 percent were black, and 11 percent were of other racial/ethnic backgrounds. It is explained in part by the atypicality of the institutions in our sample (which tended to be highly selective) and in

---

[a]See Appendix C for frequency distributions on all questionnaire items for both participants and alumnae.

part by low response rates among nonwhites. Programs that served a considerable proportion of minority students were consistently less likely to return survey questionnaires. For instance, the program with the lowest return rate both from participants (49 percent, versus 68 percent for all programs) and from alumnae (51 percent, versus 67 percent for all programs) was housed in an institution where one-third of the students were from racial/ethnic minorities.

With respect to religious background, over half of both groups were brought up as Protestants, about one-fourth as Catholics, and 17 percent as Jews. The remainder reported their religious backgrounds as "other" (3 percent) or "none" (1 percent). What is most notable here is the relatively large proportion of women in continuing education programs from Jewish backgrounds. Among women in the college population, and among adult college women, the comparable figure was only 4 percent.

The parents of women in continuing education programs were relatively well-educated. About one in three of the mothers of both participants and alumnae had at least some college, compared with only 12 percent of the mothers of adult college women. The latter were twice as likely to report that their mothers had less than a high school diploma. The majority (about one in four) in all groups said that their mothers had gone no further than graduation from high school. About 15 percent of the fathers of both participants and alumnae held a graduate or professional degree—five times the figure for fathers of adult college women. Only one-third of the fathers of participants and alumnae had less than a high school diploma, compared with 62 percent of the fathers of adult college women. About 13 percent of the participants and alumnae reported that their fathers had some college, and 11 percent that their fathers had the baccalaureate.

Since previous research suggests that working mothers exert a positive influence on their daughters' educational and occupational aspirations, it is interesting to note that 44 percent of the participants and 42 percent of the alumnae reported that their mothers had worked while they were growing up. Most commonly, these working mothers had sales or clerical jobs. Teaching, skilled occupations, and semiskilled or unskilled occupations each employed about one in ten. Only 4 percent of the mothers of participants and 7 percent of the mothers of alumnae held professional positions. About one-third of the fathers of both participants and alumnae were in business, as owners or administrators; over one in five were in skilled trades; and slightly fewer than one in five were in the professions.

About two-thirds of the participants and seven in ten alumnae were married, with about 8 percent in each group being on their second marriages. These figures correspond closely to the figures for adult college women. Most of these women had married rather young, the mean age at first marriage for both participants and alumnae being twenty-two, though the range was wide, from fifteen to forty-eight years of age. Participants were more likely than alumnae to be single (never married): 17 percent versus 11 percent. About 15 percent of the women in each group were separated or divorced, and 3 percent were widowed.

The slight differences in the median ages and marital status of the two groups account for the differences in number and ages of children. Thus, 32 percent of the participants, but only 22 percent of the alumnae, were childless. The modal number of children for both groups was two, but one in four alumnae and almost one in five participants had four or more children. Participants were almost twice as likely as alumnae to have preschool children, and alumnae were more likely than participants to have children over the age of seventeen.

The husbands of both participants and alumnae tended to be well-educated businessmen or professionals of middle-income or upper-middle-income levels. Over one in four of the husbands had a doctorate or professional degree, about three in ten had the baccalaureate, and only 15 percent had no college education. About one in three husbands was in the professions, three in ten were upper-level businessmen (administrators, owners, managers), one in ten was in teaching or educational administration, and about one in ten was in lower-level business (sales, clerical) occupations. The husbands of participants were more likely to be in the unskilled, semiskilled, or skilled trades (10 percent, versus 7 percent of the alumnae's husbands), whereas the husbands of alumnae were more likely to be retired (5 percent, versus 2 percent of the husbands of participants). Age differences were consistent with those found for the women themselves, the median age of the husbands of participants being forty-two, and of the husbands of alumnae, forty-five. The latter tended to have slightly higher incomes, a difference that may be attributed to the slight age difference. Thus, according to their wives, 36 percent of the husbands of alumnae had annual incomes of $30,000 or more, compared with 28 percent of the husbands of participants. Only about one in ten of the husbands of either group made less than $10,000.

To summarize, the typical participant in a continuing education program was a thirty-six-year-old white woman from a middle-class background, married to a forty-two-year-old business executive or professional with an income in the $10,000-19,999 range. She had two or three children of school age (though one in four had preschool children, and close to half had children of eighteen or above). Most of the participants came from Protestant backgrounds, although an unusually large proportion were Jewish. Slightly fewer than half reported that their mothers had worked while they were growing up. The alumnae were similar, allowing for slight differences accounted for by the slight age difference between the two groups. To describe the typical woman in CEW is, however, to overlook the considerable diversity in both groups: These women ranged widely in age, background, and socioeconomic status. The sample included single, divorced, and widowed women as well as married women, and minority women as well as whites.

Educational Status and Aspirations

In our survey of women in continuing education programs, items on education were designed to obtain information on past attainment, present status, and aspirations for the future and to elucidate the relationships among the three. Virtually all the respondents had completed high school (see Table 4–1), 85 percent of them with at least a B average. Indeed, about one-third of the women in both groups had made A averages. Academic success in high school was related to high degree aspirations and a strong career commitment: Of the 205 participants who had made A averages in high school, one in four was working toward the baccalaureate, and one in four was in a certificate program; 29 percent were working toward the master's degree, and 1 percent toward the Ph.D. In contrast, of the 96 participants with C averages in high school, 62 percent were working toward the baccalaureate, and 21 percent were in certificate programs; only 6 percent were working toward the master's, and none toward the Ph.D. Among those participants who planned to go into college teaching, 67 percent had As in high school, 30 percent had Bs, and only 2 percent had Cs. Women with

Table 4–1
Educational Attainment Prior to Program Contact
(Percentages)

Level of Education	Participants (N = 649)	Alumnae (N = 541)
Less than high school diploma	1	1
High school diploma	13	8
Technical or business school	7	8
Some college	30	33
Associate of Arts degree	4	4
Bachelor's degree	34	37
Master's degree	9	8
Doctorate (Ph.D., Ed.D.)	1	1
Professional degree (M.D., D.D.S., LL.B., J.D.)	0	0
Other	1	0

As in high school made up 69 percent of the respondents currently in teaching or staff positions in college, and 39 percent of teachers or staff at levels below college. Thus, it would seem that high achievement in the past makes for high aspirations and high occupational status in the present.

Returning to Table 4–1, we find that over four in five of the respondents had at least some college experience prior to their contact with a continuing education program, and close to half had a bachelor's degree or better. A larger proportion of the nonwhite (86 percent) than of the white (77 percent) participants had at least some college experience. While in college, 63 percent of the participants and 66 percent of the alumnae had maintained grade-point averages of B or better. The most popular undergraduate fields were the arts and humanities, followed by general studies or the liberal arts, education (ranking third among participants and fourth among alumnae), and the social sciences (ranking fourth among participants and third among alumnae).

Of those respondents who had not attended or completed college prior to their contact with a continuing education program, one-third cited lack of funds as the primary reason, one-fourth of the participants and one-third of the alumnae cited marriage or pregnancy, about 15 percent in each group mentioned lack of interest and motivation, and about 13 percent said they wanted to work rather than attend college.

With respect to current educational status, 42 percent of the participants and 30 percent of the alumnae were enrolled in academic programs, working toward a specific degree at the time of the survey. Of the alumnae, one-third had been in degree programs when involved in a continuing education program, and three-fourths of these women reported that they had received the degree they were working on then. Indeed, one-fourth of the alumnae not taking courses at the time of the survey or planning to take courses during the next year said that their

Table 4–2
Degree Toward Which Respondents Were Currently Working
(Percentages)

Degree Currently Working Toward	Participants (N = 271)	Alumnae Currently in Academic Programs (N = 170)
Certificate	24	13
Associate of Arts degree	8	8
Bachelor's degree	49	38
Master's degree	15	35
Doctorate (Ph.D., Ed.D.)	4	5
Professional degree (M.D., D.D.S., LL.B., J.D.)	1	2

primary reason was having already completed their degree or training. The next most frequent reason was wanting to work (15 percent), followed by being undecided about goals (11 percent).

Table 4–2 indicates the degree plans of those participants and alumnae enrolled in academic programs at the time of the survey; the largest proportion in both groups was working toward the baccalaureate, though about one-third of the alumnae were working toward the master's. Further tabulations revealed that more nonwhite (39 percent) than white (13 percent) participants were working toward the master's. Conversely, more white (24 percent) than nonwhite (11 percent) participants were in certificate programs.

Almost two-thirds of the alumnae currently in degree programs had been enrolled at least a year. In contrast, fully 70 percent of the participants indicated less than a year's involvement in the degree program. This difference is not surprising in that most participants, by definition, were in earlier stages of involvement with the program; moreover, they tended to be younger. Three-fifths of the alumnae indicated that their current academic program was in no way related to the continuing education program in which they had previously been involved. Three-fifths of the participants, however, said that their degree program *was* related, in that the continuing education program either planned or administered it (36 percent), suggested or placed them in a program run by the parent institution (18 percent), or referred them to a program in another institution (7 percent). Most of the women currently in a degree program (68 percent of the participants and 65 percent of the alumnae) were enrolled part-time. Moreover, when asked their preference, 44 percent of the participants and half the alumnae said they preferred part-time to full-time enrollment.

As Table 4–3 indicates, the most popular fields of study among those currently enrolled in degree programs were the social sciences, arts and humanities, and education (tied for third place with legal paraprofessional fields among the participants). The two reasons most frequently given for their choice of field, by both participants and alumnae, were intrinsic interest and the suitability of the field to their abilities and personalities. About three in ten of the women in both groups also mentioned job opportunities in the field, prior job or educational experience, and prior personal experience as important reasons for their choice. Fewer than one in four said that they had chosen the field because they could afford the educational and training costs or because the length of time in preparation was relatively short.

The grade-point averages of the women currently enrolled in academic programs were high. Of the participants, one in four had a grade-point average (GPA) of A, 47 percent had a GPA of B, and about one in

Table 4–3
Current Field of Study
(Percentages)

Field of Study	Participants (N = 271)	Alumnae Currently in Academic Program (N = 170)	Alumnae While in CEW (N = 190)
Arts and humanities	16	18	19
Business	9	10	4
Education	11	15	13
General studies or liberal arts	7	7	13
Health fields (non-M.D.)	8	9	5
Medicine, dentistry, law	3	4	1
Natural sciences and mathematics	3	1	2
Social sciences	22	26	15
Legal paraprofessional fields	11	1	21
Other paraprofessional fields	6	2	2
Women's studies	1	2	2
Other	4	6	3

five said they had not yet received grades. Of the alumnae, 38 percent had As, 42 percent Bs, and 13 percent had not yet received grades. Asked to indicate which of a list of personal qualities had contributed to their progress in academic programs, about four in five women in both groups cited their desire to learn. Other qualities regarded as very important were: perseverance and determination (75 percent of the participants, 80 percent of the alumnae), ambition (60 percent and 65 percent, respectively), self-discipline and organization (57 percent and 59 percent), a realistic self-assessment and self-awareness (54 percent and 59 percent), intelligence and related abilities (52 percent and 60 percent), and adaptability (51 percent and 58 percent). Relatively few checked self-confidence or assertiveness as important factors in their progress.

Asked what aspects of academic work created particular pressures or anxieties for them, close to three-fourths of the women currently enrolled in degree programs mentioned conflicting demands on their time, about three-fifths mentioned exams, and roughly half mentioned writing papers and having lengthy homework assignments. About one-third of the participants and 42 percent of the alumnae said that inadequate preparation in math and science made for difficulties. Not surprisingly, women age fifty-one and over were less apt to feel pressure because of conflicting demands on their time. Speaking before a class posed fewer difficulties for women under forty than for older women. Women over thirty, and particularly those between the age of forty-one and fifty, were more likely to cite difficulties with reading concentration, comprehension, and recall.

The degree aspirations of women currently in degree programs were high. Only 27 percent of the participants and 23 percent of the alumnae aspired to no more than the baccalaureate (compared with 65 percent of adult college women) 45 percent of both groups aspired to a master's degree (compared with 23 percent of adult college women) and 29 percent of the participants and 33 percent of the alumnae aspired to a doctoral or professional degree (compared with 7 percent of adult college women).

To summarize, most of the women in our sample came to continuing education programs with relatively strong academic records. From one-third to 40 percent were enrolled in degree or certificate programs, usually on a part-time basis. The most popular majors were the social sciences, the arts and humanities, education, and the legal paraprofessions—fields traditionally associated with women. Despite the pressure of conflicting demands on their time, most of these women made high grade-point averages in the academic program and hoped ultimately to get a graduate degree.

Factors Related to Current Educational Status

To learn more about the personal factors, experiences, and structural program characteristics related to enrollment in a degree or certificate program, we performed a series of linear multiple regression analyses, using the participant group only. (The linear multiple regression model permits one to assess the independent contribution of each significant variable.) Table 4–4 lists the variables that differentiated those enrolled in such programs from those who were not (i.e., who were involved in other aspects of continuing education, such as group counseling, workshops, and noncredit courses). Those in academic programs were more likely than others to report that their original objective in coming to continuing education was to earn a degree, certificate, or college credit; they were relatively unlikely to say that their original objective was to get counseling, testing, or information. Job dissatisfaction was a major reason for their seeking more education, and they were unlikely to be working full-time while in the program. They were less likely than participants not enrolled in academic programs to express major concern over their ability to finance their education, although they did say that costs were a major problem. In addition, those enrolled in degree or certificate progams seem in many ways to be atypical, deviating from sex-role norms. For instance, they were more inclined than others to rate themselves low on physical appearance but high on independence and to say that lack of direction was not a problem for them. Moreover, they expressed positive feelings toward the women's movement, said that their husbands approved of their working, and named nontraditional career choices such as business

Table 4–4
Factors Related to Current Enrollment in Academic Program

Variable	(R = .626) Zero-Order Correlation r	Beta Co- efficient B	(F = 25.51) F ratio
Objective: to get degree	+.53	+.436	161.56
Have financial concerns	−.14	−.144	18.50
Problem: costs	+.03	+.136	14.90
Program offers academic degree and credit courses	+.12	+.104	9.96
Self-rating: physical appearance	−.04	−.098	9.78
Objective: to receive counseling	−.07	−.099	9.51
Age of program	+.13	+.098	9.39
Problem: lack of direction	−.07	−.089	7.66
Positive attitude toward women's movement	+.08	+.087	7.11
Working full-time	−.07	−.087	6.79
Past educational attainment	−.13	−.081	5.64
Self-rating: independence	+.11	+.072	5.08
Catalyst: job dissatisfaction	+.13	+.075	4.80
Degree aspirations	−.07	−.069	4.55
Husband approves of wife's working	+.12	+.068	4.29
Nontraditional career plans	+.10	+.066	4.15

executive, business owner, scientific researcher, physician, lawyer, and college teacher or administrator.

As Tables 4–5 and 4–6 indicate, women in regular degree programs differed somewhat from those in certificate programs in that the former had higher degree aspirations, had reached a higher level educationally, and had made better grades in high school. They were also more likely to be nonwhite and to plan on entering nontraditional occupations. Those in certificate programs, on the other hand, had usually been away from school for a shorter period of time, had entered a continuing education program because they were dissatisfied with their job and wanted to prepare for a better one, and had received testing through a continuing education program.

These findings suggest the wide range of women who are served by continuing education: women who, discontent with their jobs but having a high degree of self-direction and motivation, seek to enroll in programs where they can earn a degree or credential without having to face the obstacles connected with enrolling in a traditional program to women who, because of financial strictures, may not be able to enroll in academic programs but do seek out counseling and information.

Table 4–5
Factors Related to Current Enrollment in Certificate Program

Variable	(R = .551) Zero-Order Correlation r	Beta Co-efficient B	(F = 18.47) F ratio
High degree aspirations	−.31	−.335	94.87
Contact with program: testing	+.18	+.224	36.40
Size of program	+.14	+.190	29.67
Program offers academic degrees and credit courses	+.13	+.182	26.58
Objectives: to receive counseling	−.13	−.178	25.89
Objectives: to prepare for a (better) job	+.18	+.153	17.37
Age of program	+.13	+.095	7.79
Have financial concerns	−.12	−.097	7.53
Years away from school	−.12	−.083	5.95
Problem: costs	+.08	+.093	6.39
Contact with program: group counseling	+.01	−.075	4.21
Problem: nonsupportive family	−.05	−.069	4.08
Protestant background	+.06	+.067	4.02
Catalyst: job dissatisfaction	+.07	+.074	3.99
Nontraditional career plans	+.07	+.063	3.32

Table 4–6
Factors Related to Current Enrollment in Degree Program (A.A. to Doctorate)

Variable	(R = .42) Zero-Order Correlation r	Beta Co-efficient B	(F = 14.82) F ratio
Degree aspirations	+.26	+.202	29.89
Past educational attainment	+.26	+.186	22.25
High school grades	+.19	+.121	9.89
Race/ethnicity: nonwhite	+.10	+.094	6.75
Nontraditional career plans	+.17	+.080	4.67
Problem: lack of skills	−.12	−.077	4.16
Past major field: medicine	−.06	−.071	3.91
Problem: costs	+.06	+.073	3.87
Problem: poor health	+.07	+.068	3.43

Occupational Status and Plans

Looking at the job history of the women in our sample, we find that about nine in ten had worked at some time prior to their contact with a continuing education program, most of them on a full-time basis. About 30 percent in both groups had been employed in a clerical job; 20 percent of the participants and 16 percent of the alumnae had worked as teachers, educational administrators or staff members, about three-fourths of them at the elementary or secondary level; 8 percent had been in health fields (nursing, therapy, lab technology); and 7 percent of the participants but only 5 percent of the alumnae had been in sales occupations.

At the time of the survey, over half of both groups were employed (see Table 4–7). Single women were twice as likely to be in the labor force as married women, nonwhite women were more likely to be employed than white women (69 percent and 52 percent, respectively), and younger women were more likely to be employed than older women (age thirty and under, 67 percent; age thirty-one to forty, 51 percent; age forty-one to fifty, 44 percent; and age fifty-one and over, 39 percent).

Table 4–7
Current and Future Employment
(Percentages)

	Participants		Alumnae	
	Current	*Future*	*Current*	*Future*
Employment	*(N = 649)*		*(N = 541)*	
None	47	8	46	7
Arts and writing	4	16	5	13
Business (upper-level: administration, manager, owner, consultant, accountant)	4	10	9	10
Clerical	16	3	11	1
Health fields (non-M.D.)	6	7	4	6
Professions	3	12	5	14
Sales	3	4	4	2
Social service work	4	23	4	25
Teaching and educational administration or staff	9	15	11	18
Trades	3	1	1	1

Of the women who were currently working, 70 percent of the participants and 65 percent of the alumnae were employed full-time. Full-time (versus part-time) employment was more frequent among single and previously married (separated/divorced/widowed) women than among currently married women, and among women of thirty or under (54 percent) than among older women. Although they were distributed across a number of occupational fields, the largest proportion (particularly of women age thirty or under) had clerical jobs or held teaching, administrative, or staff positions in education, mostly at the elementary and secondary levels.

These working women generally made low pay. Of those reporting incomes, the largest proportion were in the $5,000-9,999 category; about one in four had incomes of under $5,000, another one in four were in the $10,000-14,999 category, while 8 percent of the participants and 12 percent of the alumnae had incomes of $15,000 and above.[b]

The women not working at the time of the survey (almost half of both groups) were asked to indicate the primary reason for their unemployment. About three in ten said they were in school or training for work; 18 percent said they had no financial need to work; and 18 percent of the participants and 15 percent of the alumnae said that their children's needs and preferences, or their own pregnancy, kept them from working. Being in school or training was cited three times as frequently by single as by married women, and by 35 percent of the previously married women as compared with 22 percent of the currently married women. Three times as many married as single participants said they had no desire to work, whereas none of the previously married women gave this reason for nonemployment. Nonwhite women were more likely to say that they were unemployed because they were in school or training, because they lacked adequate training and experience, or because job opportunities were scarce. White women, on the other hand, more frequently said that they were unemployed because they had no financial need to work or because their children needed them at home. Of the different age groups, women age forty and under were most likely to say that they were not working because of being in school or training or because of their children's needs and preferences. Women in the forty-one to fifty age range listed having no financial need to work, being in school or training, having no desire to work, and giving precedence to their children's needs and preferences, in that order. About half of those unemployed women over fifty said that they had no financial need to work; they also checked the "other" category, which included being retired and being in poor health.

Past research has indicated that family income is a major determinant of a wife's decision to work or not to work; women whose husbands earn high incomes are less likely to work than those whose husbands earn low incomes [Astin, 1969]. To explore further the extent to which income is related to the labor force participation of women, we classified all

---

[b]It should be noted that more women reported having incomes than reported being currently employed; no doubt some had personal incomes from sources other than employment.

participants (single, currently married, separated or divorced, and widowed) as belonging to either the high-income ($10,000 and above) or the low-income (below $10,000) group; in the case of currently married women, family income was defined as the husband's income and wife's income (if any) combined. Among women in the high-income group, 53 percent were not employed, as compared with only 35 percent of those in the low-income group. Moreover, of those low-income women who were not employed at the time of the survey, 11 percent were looking for work, 45 percent were in school, and 6 percent were unemployed because of scarce job opportunities. On the other hand, unemployed high-income women were more likely to say that they had no desire or need to work, or that they were deferring to the needs and preferences of their children. In addition, 58 percent of the low-income women, but only 40 percent of the high-income women, mentioned job preparation, and 21 percent of the low-income women, but only 6 percent of the high-income women, mentioned obtaining financial aid as their objective in coming to a continuing education program. With respect to program contacts, low-income women were more likely to make use of information services, to get financial aid from the program, and to be enrolled in certificate programs, whereas high-income women were more likely to be involved in group counseling, degree programs, and noncredit classes. All these findings suggest that family income is indeed related to employment and that low-income women, if not working, come to continuing education programs specifically to acquire the skills and credentials needed to obtain employment.

Over nine in ten respondents said that they planned to work in the future, most of them full-time (see Table 4–7). About one in four planned to go into social service work, particularly counseling. The next most popular choices among participants were arts and writing, teaching and educational administration, and the professions; among alumnae they were teaching and educational administration, the professions, and arts and writing. It should be noted that those respondents who planned on jobs in education were as likely to aim for the college level as for elementary or secondary school, where women traditionally cluster. Comparing the career aspirations of women in continuing education with those of adult college women, we find that the proportions planning to go into upper-level business or education were similar but that women in CEW were more than twice as likely to aim for the professions, social service work, and arts and writing, whereas adult college women were four times as likely to plan on clerical jobs or on the health occupations other than doctoring.

To summarize, the vast majority of our sample had previous work experience. usually in such traditional women's fields as clerical work, elementary and secondary education, and the health occupations. Over half were employed at the time of the survey, generally in the same female-typed fields. Those women not currently employed usually gave as their reasons being in school or training, having no financial need to work, or giving precedence to their children's needs; the reasons varied considerably, however, depending on ethnicity, age, marital status, and family income. Almost nine in ten of the respondents said that they planned to work in the future and aimed at jobs in social service, arts and writing, education, and the professions.

Factors Relating to Current Occupational Status

As was reported above, 53 percent of the participants were employed at the time of the survey, about two-thirds of them full-time. Table 4–8 lists the personal and experiential variables found to be related to current employment. Working women were less likely than nonworking women to mention boredom at home as a catalyst to their becoming involved in continuing education and more likely to mention job dissatisfaction. They were unlikely to be enrolled in school on a full-time basis or to mention getting a degree or certificate as a major objective. It seems that currently employed participants come to continuing education programs primarily to receive information or support for possible new job placements.

Nonmarried women were more likely to be working than married women; and of the married women, those with children and with husbands who earned high incomes were less likely to be working. These findings confirm the existence of social norms that decree that mothers should not work except in cases of severe economic need. The husband's attitudes seem to be particularly important in determining the wife's employment; thus, working women were more likely than nonworking women to say that their husbands approved of their working. However, these same husbands were less likely to be supportive of the interests and activities of their wives in continuing education.

As was mentioned earlier, the research literature suggests that working mothers exert a strong influence on the lives of their daughters. This suggestion is supported by the connection between the participant's having had a working mother while she was growing up and her present status: being employed and at the same time participating in a continuing education program. The working mother's absence from the home may foster great independence, as is indicated by the employed participant's tendency to rate herself high on independence. In this context, it is also significant that these working women had liberal attitudes about how old the children should be before the mother returns to work or to school.

Table 4–8
Factors Related to Current Employment

Variable	(R = .620) Zero-Order Correlation r	Beta Co-efficient B	(F = 24.76) F ratio
Catalyst: bored at home	−.31	−.235	52.48
Enrolled full-time	−.13	−.217	41.62
Husband approves of wife's working	+.32	+.204	29.80
Conservative view about mothers' working/ going to school	−.26	−.142	17.35
Objective: to get degree	−.09	−.13	14.14
Catalyst: job dissatisfaction	+.22	+.13	13.12
Number of children	−.28	−.12	10.01
Husband is supportive	−.01	−.10	9.08
Husband's income	−.26	−.11	8.58
Mother worked while participant was growing up	+.13	+.09	8.58
Currently married	−.26	−.11	8.33
High school grades	−.03	−.09	8.32
Jewish background	−.16	−.08	6.55
Past major field: health fields (non-M.D.)	+.07	+.07	4.22
Self-rating: independence	+.15	+.06	3.42

Self-Ratings and Attitudes

The survey questionnaire included a number of items dealing with the respondent's self-concept and her attitudes toward marriage, work, and the women's movement. Asked to rate themselves on a list of traits as "compared with the average woman of your own age," both participants and alumnae emerged as having a very positive self-image (Table 4–9). Thus, at least two-thirds rated themselves as above average or in the top 10 percent in effectiveness on the job, independence, academic ability, physical appearance, and drive to achieve. Indeed, on only four traits—mathematical ability, athletic ability, public speaking ability, and artistic ability—did as many as three-fifths of the respondents rate themselves as no better than average; and even in those cases, they tended to give themselves higher ratings than did adult college women.

Both participants and alumnae were particularly likely to give themselves high ratings on those qualities that make for academic and occupational success: academic ability, intellectual self-confidence, writing ability, leadership, job effectiveness, assertiveness, independence, and originality. They were no more likely than adult college women, however, to rate themselves high on drive to achieve: about two-thirds said they

Table 4–9
Self-Ratings
(Percentages)

Trait	Participants (N = 649)			Alumnae (N = 541)		
	Highest 10%	*Above Average*	*Total*	*Highest 10%*	*Above Average*	*Total*
Physical appearance	17	51	68	18	53	71
Social self-confidence	13	42	55	14	47	61
Intellectual self-confidence	15	50	65	19	52	71
Sensitivity to criticism	13	32	45	9	32	41
Popularity with women	9	39	48	7	38	45
Popularity with men	9	42	51	9	40	49
Leadership	14	43	57	15	43	58
Academic ability	20	49	69	21	49	70
Effectiveness on job	30	53	83	29	52	81
Homemaking ability	16	35	51	15	38	53
Success as mother	23	45	68	22	47	69
Success as wife	22	37	59	20	37	57
Athletic ability	6	26	32	6	21	27
Drive to achieve	21	45	66	20	47	67
Originality	17	39	56	18	39	57
Cheerfulness	16	43	59	17	43	60
Assertiveness	13	38	51	12	41	53
Mental and emotional well-being	16	41	57	19	35	54
Public speaking ability	9	29	38	11	29	40
Writing ability	15	39	54	17	41	58
Artistic ability	11	29	40	12	28	40
Mathematical ability	6	19	25	4	23	27
Independence	27	45	72	24	51	75
Physical stamina	12	39	51	17	34	51

were above average or in the top 10 percent. Various subgroups within the participant sample differed slightly in their ratings. For instance, nonwhite women were almost twice as likely as white women to rate themselves in the top 10 percent on independence. Single and separated, divorced, or widowed women were more likely than were currently married women to rate themselves high on both independence and cheerfulness.

About half the respondents rated themselves high on homemaking ability; 59 percent of the participants and 57 percent of the alumnae rated themselves high on success as a wife; and two-thirds of both groups rated themselves high on success as a mother. Again, there were differences among the subgroups, with married women rating themselves in the top

10 percent on success as a mother slightly more often than did separated, divorced, or widowed women. On homemaking ability they rated themselves in the top 10 percent three times as often as single women, and on success as a wife five times as often as separated, divorced, or widowed women. These differences make good sense in view of the probably different experiences of the three groups.

Consistent with the tendency to see themselves as successful wives and mothers, three-fourths of the respondents regarded their marriages (or, in the case of nonmarried women, their current love relationships) as fairly or very happy. Only 12 percent of the participants and 10 percent of the alumnae said they had an unhappy marriage or love relationship. The remainder reported no current relationship. About one-third of the respondents indicated that their marriage had improved as a result of the women's movement; on the other hand, 17 percent of the participants and 13 percent of the alumnae said that their marriages had been threatened or dissolved as a result. Describing their husbands' attitude toward their participation in a CEW program, 62 percent of the participants and 57 percent of the alumnae said it was very supportive, 20 percent of the participants and 23 percent of the alumnae said it was somewhat supportive, and 5 percent of the participants and 7 percent of the alumnae said it was not supportive.

Additional analyses comparing those participants who perceived their husbands as being supportive of their participation in a continuing education program with those who perceived their husbands as neutral or not supportive indicate that 38 percent of the latter group, compared with only 6 percent of the former, characterized their marriages as unhappy. Moreover, 30 percent of the women with nonsupportive husbands, compared with 8 percent of those with supportive husbands, said that during their contact with a continuing education program, they had experienced marital tensions and difficulties. Finally, one in five women with nonsupportive spouses, compared with only 6 percent of those with supportive ones, rated themselves below average on success as a wife. It should be pointed out that these relationships between the husband's supportiveness and marital satisfaction or problems are concomitant and do not necessarily imply cause and effect. Nonetheless, it is understandable that when the husband is sympathetic to and supportive of his wife's interests and needs, she is more likely to view the marriage as a happy one and to see herself as a successful wife. (These relationships are discussed in greater detail in Chapter 5.)

In addition, looking only at those participants who had children, one finds that guilt about neglecting children while in the continuing education program was mentioned as a very important problem by 6 percent of the married women and by 7 percent of the separated, divorced, or widowed women. Mothers of preschool children were more likely than mothers of older children to express these guilt feelings. Those mothers in the sample of participants who said that it was appropriate for a woman to return to work or to school at any time after she has borne a child were more likely than mothers with more conservative attitudes on this issue to have been away from school for five years or less; 70 percent of the more liberal mothers had dropped out of school for no longer than that time. Comparing the attitudes of different age groups of participants, and of women with and without children, on the same issue, we found that women without children tended to take the more liberal view, perhaps because they had not experienced the demands and the sense of responsibility that one feels in actually caring for children. Indeed, younger women with children were much more liberal in their views than were older women: 43 percent of the women age thirty or under felt it was appropriate for a mother of preschool children to engage in activities outside the home such as education or work, compared with only 13 percent of the women over fifty. This difference may reflect a generational rather than an age change. That is, attitudes toward working mothers have become more liberal over the last few decades.

The sense of competence, drive, and independence revealed in the self-ratings is confirmed by the degree of career commitment manifested by both participants and alumnae; just over three-fourths of both groups indicated that having a career in addition to being a wife and mother was important or very important to their self-fulfillment. About 14 percent in each group was neutral on the subject. Only 9 percent of the participants and 10 percent of the alumnae said that a career was unimportant to them. Some differences among subgroups of participants emerge. Single women were more likely than were currently married women to regard a career as important. Two-thirds of the women age thirty or under, 54 percent of those in the age thirty-one to forty group, and only 37 percent of those over forty attached great importance to having a career. Again, these differences may be generational: Younger women have grown up in a social milieu generally more favorable toward careers for women and less insistent about traditional marriages and large families.

Slightly more than half of the respondents reported unqualified positive feelings toward the women's movement, slightly less than half had mixed reactions, and only 4 percent of the participants and 2 percent of the alumnae had negative feelings. Positive feelings were more frequent among participants of thirty years or under (63 percent) than among those age thirty-one to forty (52 percent) or forty-one and older (46 percent). Conversely, women over forty were more likely to report definite negative feelings than were younger women. Single women were the most likely to have positive feelings (though this may result from the age factor), and married women were the most likely to have mixed reactions. The three most frequently cited effects of the women's movement, in descending order, were: greater awareness of issues concerning women; concern with encouraging girls to consider all career alternatives, including "men's" jobs; and increased respect for and understanding of women.

To summarize, women who are or have been in continuing education programs generally see themselves as competent and successful in several spheres: work, academia, and the home. Three-fourths report that their marriages are happy, and an equal fraction say that having a career, in addition to being a wife and mother, is important to their sense of self-fulfillment. Half of the respondents were favorable toward the women's movement, slightly less than half had mixed reactions, and only a handful were definitely negative.

To learn more about the personal and experiential characteristics of the more outstanding members of this generally ambitious and able group of women, we carried out some additional analyses, using the linear multiple regression model, on three subgroups: career-oriented women, career-innovative women, and active alumnae.

Career-Oriented Women

Slightly over half of the participants indicated that it was very important to their self-fulfillment to have a career in addition to being wives and mothers. To learn more about the factors related to a high degree of career commitment, we performed a linear multiple regression analysis comparing this group with women who attached less importance to having a career. As Table 4–10 indicates, the career-oriented woman was likely to plan on entering a nontraditional field, was liberal in her views as to what age children should be when the mother goes off to school or work, had a positive attitude toward the women's movement, and rated herself high on intellectual self-confidence. She was inclined to feel restless and discontent with her life and to enter a continuing education program to escape from the boredom of home. Moreover, she had been away from school a relatively short time. Her experiences in the program contributed to her self-awareness and insight. Not only was she more likely than the less career-oriented woman to have worked in the past, but also she was more likely to be employed while in the continuing education program; and she reported that her husband approved of her working. The picture that emerges of the career-oriented woman is of an active and self-confident person, both liberal and liberated, whose abilities and energies render her dissatisfied with the prospect of confining her life to the home.

Table 4-10
Characteristics of Career-Oriented Women

Variable	(R = .647) Zero-Order Correlation r	Beta Co-efficient B	(F = 30.37) F ratio
Nontraditional career plans	+.18	+.213	44.58
Conservative view about mothers' working/going to school	−.43	−.209	37.03
Positive attitude toward women's movement	+.32	+.170	27.91
Husband approves of wife's working	+.33	+.157	19.94
Years away from school	−.32	−.142	19.35
Catalyst: boredom at home	+.04	+.119	12.42
Change: greater self-awareness	+.10	+.085	7.58
Husband's income	−.26	−.087	7.14
Intellectual self-confidence	+.12	+.075	5.93
Currently working	+.23	+.082	5.49
Past major field: business	−.09	−.067	4.72
Did not work in past	−.26	−.063	3.70
Protestant background	−.02	−.056	3.39
Feeling: restless and discontent	+.17	+.058	3.30
Marital satisfaction	−.09	−.056	3.01

Career-Innovative Women

Another group of women whom we regarded as especially interesting were those who planned to enter occupations generally regarded as "off limits" to women: business executive or owner, scientific researcher, physician, lawyer, college teacher or administrator. As Table 4-11 shows, these women were liberal in their views about how old children should be when the mother goes to work or back to school. Moreover, they made good grades in college and had been away from school a relatively short period of time. Job dissatisfaction was a catalyst in their coming to continuing education.

Among the respondents who named nontraditional career choices were women in academic programs, working toward regular degrees or toward certificates. The earlier analysis of women in certificate programs indicated that they had low degree aspirations, yet choosing a nontraditional career was related to high degree aspirations. It would seem then, that among women currently working toward certificates, those with high degree aspirations were more likely to choose innovative careers than were those who planned to terminate their education after receiving the certificate. These women viewed the certificate only as an interim arrangement. For example, women in the legal assistant program were

Table 4–11
Characteristics of Career-Innovative Women

Variable	(R = .395) Zero-Order Correlation r	Beta Co-efficient B	(F = 10.74) F ratio
Conservative view about mother's working/ going to school	−.23	−.14	13.49
College grades	+.17	+.12	9.79
Degree aspirations	+.17	+.12	8.84
Working toward certificate	+.07	+.10	6.81
Working toward regular degree	+.17	+.09	6.25
Past major field: arts and humanities	+.17	+.09	5.90
Husband is supportive	+.10	+.08	4.45
Self-rating: leadership	+.09	+.08	4.34
Catalyst: job dissatisfaction	+.16	+.07	3.53
Years away from school	−.17	−.07	3.31
Jewish background	−.09	−.06	3.09

taking intensive training so that they would qualify to work as legal assistants; if, after they had been on the job for a while, they felt that they still had the interest and the talent to pursue legal training, they planned to enter law school and eventually become lawyers.

As was the case with career-oriented women, having a supportive husband was important to career-innovative women. These women also tended to rate themselves high on their leadership abilities.

Active Alumnae

The women defined as *active alumnae* are those alumnae who, at the time of the survey, indicated that they were employed (54 percent) or in an academic program, pursuing either a certificate or a regular degree (30 percent); some women were doing both. Only about 30 percent of the alumnae were neither working nor enrolled in academic programs.

As Table 4–12 indicates, the active alumnae (as opposed to the relatively inactive ones) were young women who did not have preschool children and whose husbands approved of their working. Their objectives in coming to the continuing education program had been to get a degree and prepare for a better job; they reported that a major problem while in the program was lack of energy, but they were unlikely to mention lack of skills as a problem; and they felt that one outcome of CEW was to give them greater focus and direction. They were unlikely to express financial concerns. These women were career-oriented and had liberal views about the mother's working or going to school while her children were young. Their high level of activity is evidenced by their having done volunteer work in the past. They were more likely than were inactive alumnae to say that the women's movement had to some degree threatened their marriages but not that it made them feel restless and discontent with their lives—hardly surprising in view of their involvement in activities outside the home.

Table 4–12
Characteristics of Active Alumnae

Variable	(R = .564) Zero-Order Correlation r	Beta Co-efficient B	(F = 12.795) F ratio
Husband approves of wife's working	+.32	+.210	28.48
Objectives: to get degree	+.28	+.161	15.80
Age of participant	−.26	−.158	13.99
Problem: lack of skills	−.11	−.126	10.63
Have financial concerns	−.14	−.119	10.26
Feeling: restless and discontent	−.14	−.119	9.92
Program offers credit courses and academic degrees	−.04	−.115	8.95
Problem: lack of energy	+.11	+.104	7.19
Have preschool children	.00	−.101	6.66
Did volunteer work	+.03	+.079	4.58
Changes: focus and direction	+.12	+.078	4.18
Feeling: marriage has been threatened	+.04	+.074	3.99
Career-oriented	+.29	+.083	3.85
Conservative view about mothers' working and/or going to school	−.21	−.078	3.43
Protestant background	−.09	−.069	3.37
Objective: to prepare for (better) job	+.24	+.076	3.32
Mother worked while participant was growing up	+.12	+.067	3.25

These findings make it clear that, within the group of women who become involved in continuing education, there are great differences with respect to career orientation and attitudes about mothers who work while their children are young. These views differentiate those women who choose to become involved in further education or in the world of work from those who do not so choose. In addition, the analysis confirms findings from other studies with different samples that (1) a woman whose mother worked is more likely herself to work; and (2) a woman whose husband makes a high income is less likely to work than a woman with a similar educational background whose husband earns a relatively low income.

Experiences in CEW Programs

Finally, the questionnaire elicited information on women in relation to continuing education programs: their objectives in entering the programs, the catalytic events that had preceded their entry, their contacts with various program components and services, the structural and personal obstacles they encountered during their participation in CEW, outcomes and effects, recommendations for improving the program, and factors related to satisfaction with the program.

As Table 4–13 indicates, the three objectives ranked most important, cited by almost equal proportions of participants and alumnae, were (1) to become more educated (63 percent and 62 percent, respectively), (2) to achieve independence and a sense of identity (44 percent and 43 percent), and (3) to prepare for a better job (44 percent and 42 percent). About one-third of the respondents said that they came to get counseling and information and to develop skills that would make them more effective in the family and community. Alumnae were somewhat more likely than were participants to say they aimed at receiving a degree, certificate, or college credit and at assessing themselves academically, whereas participants were more likely to want to make contact with other people. Only about one in ten respondents was concerned with obtaining financial assistance or with becoming involved in women's programs and issues.

Table 4–13
Objectives in Coming to CEW
(Percentages)

Objective	Participants (N = 649)	Alumnae (N = 541)
To become more educated	63	62
To achieve independence and a sense of identity	44	43
To prepare for a better job	44	42
To receive counseling, testing, information	35	31
To develop skills to become more effective in family/community	34	33
To receive a degree/certificate/college credit	29	35
To assess self academically	26	31
To make contact with other people	24	20
To obtain financial assistance	10	8
To be involved in women's programs and issues	10	8

Objectives varied somewhat depending on the age, marital status, and income level of participants. Thus, half the single women and 58 percent of the separated, divorced, or widowed women cited job preparation as an important objective, though it was less important to married women. This goal was also more important to women of forty or under than to older women. Younger women were also more likely to aim at receiving a degree. The goal of obtaining financial aid was more important to women of thirty and under, to the single and the previously married, and to minority women than it was to the older married white participants. Job preparation was a very important objective to 58 percent of low-income women (family income under $10,000), compared with 40 percent of the high-income women; and 21 percent of the low-income women cited obtaining financial assistance as an important objective, compared with only 6 percent of the high-income women.

The majority of respondents cited the program's offerings as a major catalyst in their decision to enter a continuing education program (see Table 4–14). The next most important catalyst was encouragement and recommendations from other people. Job dissatisfaction and boredom at home were each cited as factors in the respondents' decision by roughly one-fifth of both groups. Alumnae were slightly more likely than were participants to mention the lessening of home responsibilities—understandable, since their children tended to be slightly older. Such catalytic factors as the availability of funds, family or marital problems, and a move to a new location were mentioned by about one in ten respondents, and 4 percent of each group mentioned a serious illness or death in the family.

Table 4–14
Major Catalysts in Coming to CEW
(Percentages)

Catalyst	Participants (N = 649)	Alumnae (N = 541)
Program's offerings	61	56
Encouragement/recommendations from others	33	29
Dissatisfied with job	22	20
Bored at home	18	21
Lessening of home responsibilities	16	20
Availability of funds	13	10
Family/marital problems	10	9
My move to this location/community	7	4
Serious illness/death in family	4	4

Of more significance were differences by age, marital status, and race. Thus, those participants who were more likely to be working were also more likely to report job dissatisfaction as a catalyst—i.e., younger women

(32 percent) and the single (36 percent) or the separated, divorced, or widowed (31 percent). Conversely, 22 percent of the thirty-one to forty-year-olds, 21 percent of the above-fifty-year-olds, and one in five of the married women mentioned boredom at home as important.

Previously married women (separated/divorced/widowed) were five times as likely as were married participants to cite family and marital problems as a catalyst. These women were also much more likely to indicate that job preparation was their primary objective in entering a continuing education program. In short, there emerges the classic picture of the woman who—because of marital strains, divorce, or bereavement—is thrown upon her own resources and must prepare herself for a job. Finally, twice as many nonwhite as white women mentioned marital and family problems as a catalytic factor; they, and nonmarried women as well, were also more likely to say that the availability of funds influenced their decision.

The program components with which the individual student has contact will depend, of course, on the services available in a specific program. Nonetheless, it is instructive to get some overall sense of the most frequently utilized features of a program. Of the participants, about two-thirds had in the past made use of information services; 23 percent were doing so at the time of the survey. Another one in four came to the programs for referral and testing. Twelve percent had received either individual or group counseling, and another 10 percent were currently being counseled. With respect to classes, 11 percent were enrolled in degree programs, 7 percent were in certificate programs, 14 percent were taking credit courses or seminars, 21 percent were taking noncredit courses, 5 percent were participating in workshops, and 3 percent were taking in-service training, either within the program or at an outside agency. Only 4 percent currently, and 6 percent in the past, had received financial aid through CEW. Low-income women were more likely to be involved in informational services, financial aid, or certificate programs, whereas high-income women were more likely to be involved in group counseling, degree programs, or noncredit courses.

As Table 4–15 indicates, the three problems most frequently cited as very important during participation in CEW were all program-related: the time of day that classes were offered (mentioned by close to half of both groups), location, distance, and transportation (mentioned by over one in four), and costs (again, mentioned by one in four). The various pressures connected with being in school and at the same time trying to carry out other duties also created problems for many respondents; close to one in four mentioned lack of time, job responsibilities, and family obligations as obstacles. Other problems were more closely connected with the respondent's competencies, motivation, and feelings: lack of specific skills and abilities (cited by 15 percent of the participants and 17 percent of the alumnae), lack of direction or purpose (15 percent and 16 percent, respectively), lack of self-confidence (12 percent and 10 percent), lack of energy and physical endurance (11 percent and 13 percent), guilt about money (9 percent and 7 percent), and guilt about neglect of children (8 percent and 7 percent). It is interesting to note that only 5 percent of the participants and 6 percent of the alumnae regarded nonsupportive family attitudes as a problem.

Table 4–15
Problems Encountered during Participation in CEW
(Percentages)

Problem	Participants (N = 649)	Alumnae (N = 541)
Time of day classes offered	46	46
Location, distance, transportation	26	29
Costs	26	28
Lack of time	20	24
Job responsibilities	19	22
Family obligations	18	19
Lack of specific skills/abilities	15	17
Lack of direction/purpose	15	16
Lack of self-confidence	12	10
Lack of energy, physical endurance	11	13
Guilt about money	9	7
Guilt about neglect of children	8	7
Negative experience with instructor	8	9
Medical reasons	5	6
Nonsupportive family attitudes	5	6
Other	2	3

Age, marital status, and race were related to the nature of the problems that participants faced. Thus, women under age thirty-one and single or previously married women were more likely than were older and currently married women to regard costs as a problem. Women age thirty-one to forty and married women were the most likely to have conflicts as a result of family obligations, whereas women age forty-one to fifty and single women were the most likely to report major difficulties due to job responsibilities. Women age fifty-one and over were less likely to feel heavy time pressures, whereas women under forty were more likely to experience guilt over money or neglect of children. Lack of specific skills was twice as likely to be mentioned as a problem by minority women as by white women.

Of those women currently enrolled in degree or certificate programs, 21 percent of the participants and 13 percent of the alumnae expressed major concern over their ability to finance their education. Almost half of the alumnae, but only a third of the participants, said they had no such anxiety over finances, an understandable difference considering the higher incomes of the alumnae's husbands.

In reply to an item on the extent to which the continuing education program had influenced various personal changes, most respondents indicated positive effects (Table 4–16). For instance, two in five said that the program had increased their self-awareness and insight; one third said it had made them more open to ideas and people; 32 percent of the participants and 38 percent of the alumnae mentioned increased confidence and self-esteem; and over one in four said that it had provided focus and direction, made them happier people, informed them of alternatives and options, and made them feel better educated. An increased liking and respect for other women was mentioned by 24 percent of both groups. More alumnae than participants said that the program had helped them to develop their employable skills (20 percent versus 13 percent) or motivated them to seek employment (13 percent versus 5 percent). Single and previously married women were twice as likely as married women to mention the development of employable skills, and three times as likely to mention having been influenced to seek employment—relationships consistent with the tendency of nonmarried women to cite employment-related objectives. Fewer than 4 percent of either participants or alumnae mentioned negative changes—confusion over goals, fatigue and depression, a loss of self-confidence, or the conviction that "my place is at home"—resulting from the continuing education program.

Respondents also noted the effects of their participation in CEW on family, job, and interpersonal relationships (Table 4–17). The most frequently mentioned outcome, cited by 54 percent of the participants and 61 percent of the alumnae, was that their children's respect and regard for them had increased; in addition, slightly over half said that they had gained the respect of other people. About one-third in both groups—but more alumnae than participants—said that their involvement had led to improved marital relations and inproved job status and that it had drawn the family closer together and at the same time made them more self-reliant and organized. But the same fraction said also that their participation meant they had less time for social life. In most cases, larger proportions of alumnae than of participants mentioned specific changes, including the family's having less time together, marital tensions and difficulties, and the disapproval or jealousy of friends and neighbors. Perhaps the greater tendency of alumnae to perceive change as a result of

Table 4–16
Changes Resulting from Participation in CEW
(Percentages)

Change	Participants (N = 649)	Alumnae (N = 541)
Increased self-awareness, insight	39	40
I have become more open to ideas, people	36	37
Gave me confidence, increased self-esteem	32	38
Provided focus and direction	32	30
Provided catalyst for further education	31	35
I am a happier person	31	31
Informed me of alternatives, options	30	29
I feel better educated	29	36
Increased my liking and respect for other women	24	24
I have developed employable skills	13	20
Caused me to seek employment	5	13
I feel more confused about my goals	3	3
I feel tired and depressed	2	1
Decreased my self-confidence	2	1
Made me decide my place is at home	1	1

the program results from their having had more opportunity to assess long-term change. The only exceptions to these differences in perception of change involve resentment and distress on the part of the children, reported by 4 percent in each group, and the resentment or disapproval of coworkers, mentioned by 8 percent of the participants but only 5 percent of the alumnae. One difference in perceived effects was related to age of the participant: Over three in five of the women forty-one or older indicated that their children's respect for them had increased, compared with only half of the women age thirty-one to forty and slightly over one-third of those age thirty or less. The explanation is probably that older women tend to have children mature enough to understand and appreciate their mother's efforts to further her education. The increased respect of the children may, however, be expressed at a distance, since fewer of them live at home with their parents.

In making recommendations for improvement in the continuing education programs, about one in five respondents in both groups indicated that much change was needed in the following areas: increased publicity, more locations, more choices of time that services are offered, increased funding and staffing, and enrollment of a wider population (men, younger women, disadvantaged women). Just as they were more inclined to perceive greater program effects, so alumnae were more likely than were participants to believe that considerable change was needed. For instance, provision or improvement of job placement services was

Table 4–17
Effects of Participation in CEW
(Percentages)

Effect	Participants (N = 649)	Alumnae (N = 541)
Children's respect and regard toward me increased	54	61
Other people respect me more	51	53
Marital relations improved	35	37
Less time for social life	35	38
Has improved my status on job	34	39
Family is closer, talks things over more	34	37
Family is more self-reliant and organized	32	42
Family has less time together	22	30
Marital tensions and difficulties	13	18
Some friends or neighbors disapproving or jealous	11	17
Co-workers resent or disapprove	8	5
Children upset, resent my involvement	4	4

cited by 29 percent of the alumnae but only 20 percent of the participants; better educational or occupational information was cited by 26 percent of the alumnae and 22 percent of the participants. The differences on these two items are not surprising, since alumnae are more likely to be searching for jobs in which they can apply what they gained in CEW. Understandable as well is their greater emphasis on the need for the evaluation of courses and services for follow-up on students (25 percent of the alumnae, 19 percent of the participants) and on the need for counseling that is more responsive to the needs of the individual (22 percent and 17 percent, respectively). About one in five alumnae, but only 17 percent of the participants, wanted lower tuitions and more financial aid. Other items on which the two groups differed were the need for a greater variety of courses (23 percent of the alumnae, 19 percent of the participants), for child-care facilities (15 percent of the alumnae, 11 percent of the participants), and for improvement in the quality of teachers and speakers (12 percent and 9 percent, respectively). Relatively few in either group were much concerned about the program's providing more contact among participants or becoming more independent of the parent institution's facilities and staff.

In general, women involved in CEW expressed satisfaction with the program: 45 percent of the participants and 43 percent of the alumnae indicated they were very satisfied, another 36 percent of the participants and 35 percent of the alumnae said they were somewhat satisfied, and only 10 percent of the participants and 11 percent of the alumnae indicated they were somewhat or very dissatisfied. The remainder were neutral.

To summarize, most women come to continuing education programs to get more education; personal fulfillment and job preparation are also important objectives. The chief catalysts in their involvement are the program's offerings and encouragement or recommendations from other people. Information services and course offerings (credit and noncredit) were the program components used most frequently; in addition, large proportions of both groups enrolled in degree or certificate programs, or became involved in group or individual counseling. Program-related obstacles such as costs and the scheduling and location of classes were likely to present problems. Many women perceived changes in themselves as a result of the program, including a growth in self-awareness, a greater openness to people and ideas, and increased confidence and self-esteem. Alumnae were somewhat more likely than were participants to say that their children and other people had come to respect them more as a result of the program, their marriage had improved, their family had become more self-reliant and at the same time closer, and their job status had improved. In their recommendations for improvement, the women focused both on changing those aspects of the program that had constituted barriers for them and on the need for better educational and occupational information and for job placement services.

Factors Related to Satisfaction with the Program

Looking just at the participants, we find that those women who expressed satisfaction with the program were also more likely than dissatisfied women to report positive program effects: greater focus and direction, increased self-awareness, increased confidence, and more respect for other women (Table 4–18). In contrast, those women who were less than satisfied were also more likely to report that costs and a lack of direction or purpose constituted problems for them during their participation in the program. Satisfied women tended to be more confident of their leadership abilities but less so of their intellectual skills and to have high degree aspirations; they were not likely to be currently working. The explanation here may be that women who are in general more critical and who regard themselves as intellectual are also more likely to be critical of the programs and thus less than satisfied with them. Conversely, it may be that the programs are better able to satisfy those women who come with a need for personal growth and for a more clearly defined focus than those women who want simply to get a degree and prepare for careers.

Women satisfied with the program were found to be older, to have more children, to have been away from school longer, and to have made use of the program's individual counseling services. The picture that emerges is that of a woman who has been family-oriented in the past, who

Table 4–18
Factors Related to Satisfaction with CEW

Variable	(R = .54) Zero-Order Correlation r	Beta Co-efficient B	(F = 21.36) F ratio
Change: greater focus and direction	+.37	+.16	15.83
Change: greater self-awareness	+.40	+.17	14.19
Problem: lack of direction	−.11	−.12	12.07
Change: greater self-confidence	+.40	+.15	11.72
Age of participant	+.14	+.10	8.11
Change: greater respect for other women	+.32	+.11	7.29
Self-rating: intellectual self-confidence	−.06	−.09	6.87
Self-rating: leadership	+.13	+.08	4.79
Degree aspirations	+.07	+.07	4.39
Problem: costs	−.06	−.06	3.48
Currently working	−.10	−.06	3.24

has not worked, and who does not have strong occupational interests. The more career-oriented woman may be less inclined to feel satisfied with her experience in the program, even though it has enabled her to pursue her occupational interest without having to face the barriers that usually confront adults in traditional institutions.

Note

1. Information on women in the general college population was drawn from *The American Freshman: National Norms for Fall 1974* [Astin et al., 1974]. Data on adult college women were provided by special tabulations abstracted from the freshman national norms.

5

Home Life of Women in Continuing Education

Joseph Katz

In approaching the study of continuing education programs, we were especially interested in learning how going to school affects the family life of the adult woman student. Some observers have voiced the fear that the return to education disrupts husband-wife relationships and affects children negatively. Therefore we sought answers to such questions as:

- Are husbands supportive of the educational and occupational aspirations of their wives, and what are the limits to their support?
- Does the wife's return to school lead to tensions and conflicts between the partners?
- Does mother's being in school make children feel neglected, lead to tensions between mother and child, and otherwise adversely affect children's behavior and attitudes?

There are many who think that we have entered a period in which male and female roles are being redefined in a revolutionary way. Education is both a vehicle for and an expression of the changes occurring in the society at large. Our study of continuing education clearly demonstrates the validity of this proposition.

This chapter is based both on responses to the survey questionnaire and on interviews conducted with women students and their families in the fifteen continuing education programs.[a] Two-hundred-and-twelve currently enrolled students (three-fourths of them married), seventy-seven husbands, and eighty-eight children were interviewed. The children ranged in age from nine to eighteen years, with 69 percent being under thirteen. Questionnaires were returned by 427 married women students and 154 of their spouses; whenever percentages are cited, they refer to questionnaire responses.

The interviews with the families were conducted in the women's own homes. The reception given to the interviewers was cordial, reflecting the warmth which the students felt about their programs. Given the nature of our sample, it is not surprising that the homes were comfortable and

[a]Unlike Chapter 4, which gives data on the entire group of survey respondents, this chapter is based primarily on data obtained from the married women, with a small section on separated and divorced women. This explains any seeming discrepancies in reported percentages between this chapter and the previous one.

located in well-cared-for neighborhoods. The husband, the wife, and each child were interviewed separately. The younger children tended to approach the interviews with mixed excitement and anxiety. It was difficult to confine the interviews to the allotted time span (approximately one hour), particularly in the case of the women and their husbands, who viewed the return to education as an important part of their lives. Far more was involved than just going to school: Changes in the way in which the family lived, in wife-husband relations, in family activities, in the woman's self-concept, in the husband's sense of his role and personal aspirations, and in the children's perceptions of their mother were reported. The families talked volubly, would gladly have continued the discussion, and perhaps needed to continue in order to come to grips with an experience that they saw as changing their lives. The interviewers were treated as special guests, and the whole occasion had a festive air.

Common Characteristics of Married Women Students

The return to school of the married women in our study—41 percent of whom were more than forty years old—must be viewed against the background of their very busy lives. About seven in ten had two or more children, and two-thirds of these children were no more than twelve years old. In addition, nearly half of the wives were currently employed, the majority full-time. No wonder that 70 percent said that conflicting demands on their time was a source of stress. (Interestingly, 57 percent of the single women registered the same complaint.) Nonetheless, they did not see their many activities as interfering with their lives at home. About two-thirds described themselves as successful beyond the average in their roles as wives and mothers. Only one in five said she joined the continuing education program primarily out of boredom with her home life; the intrinsic appeal of the program was much more likely to be the catalyst.

Women who return to education have much in common with each other. Reading interviews collected in many different parts of the country, one is struck by the similarities in the reports, sometimes even to the point of identical wording, as if these people had talked together and arrived at a common vocabulary. The most striking similarities were the enthusiasm expressed for learning and the reports of considerably increased self-esteem. Many of the interviewees said simply, "I like myself better." Whether the woman had earlier attended the best available college or gone no further than high school, whether she was highly able or only moderately so, whether she was upper-class or lower-class, she stressed her excitement about learning and her sense of greater strength. As one interviewee put it, "I feel I can push boulders."

The women spoke with zest about their experiences in the classroom. Those interviewed near the end of the school year said they were sorry it was coming to an end. They felt that they were learning much more efficiently than they had during their previous college days. Of the married women currently in courses where grades were given, 37 percent made A averages, and only 6 percent made C averages, whereas in their prior college work, only 16 percent had received A averages, and 22 percent C averages. Not only were they now studying better, but also they felt that they were understanding much more. Comparing themselves with their younger classmates, the interviewees saw themselves as more serious, dedicated, and motivated, more aware of alternative views, and more willing to challenge their professors. In the questionnaire sample over two-thirds described themselves as above average in academic ability, intellectual self-confidence, and independence. The continuing education program had helped them to develop those qualities. Seventy-five percent stated that they had become happier persons as a result of their participation in the program. Even higher percentages reported increases in self-esteem, self-awareness, and openness to new ideas and people. Many of the interviewees had had doubts about their mental abilities and hesitated before putting themselves to the test by enrolling in the program. Even women who had previously attended elite colleges said that for the first time they were using their minds, while before their learning had been much more passive.

This constitutes something of a puzzle, particularly in the case of those women who had previously attended prestigious small colleges where the faculty was able, dedicated to teaching, and supportive of originality. Some of the reported differences between then and now may be attributable to natural developmental patterns: It is possible that girls in late adolescence are troubled by questions about their own worth and about what others think of them, anxious about their physical appearance, guilty because they are hanging onto childhood and at the same time struggling against their dependency. If so, such inner turmoil may interfere with learning. A further explanation lies in the intervening experiences these women have had: their lives with husbands and children, their work, their social and community activities. Through these experiences they have acquired a much firmer sense of the reality of external objects, have been kindly and unkindly affected by them, and have developed a more detailed perception of and respect for what exists outside of their own bodies and minds.

Since they last attended school many of these women had become managers of households, wage earners (44 percent were currently employed, 89 percent had been employed at some time in the past), participants in the tasks and manipulations of working life, mothers dealing with the instinctiveness and power of young children, and women who could understand adult men as fallible and at times even childlike human beings. These experiences, along with their considerably enlarged and objectified sense of reality, have enabled them to grasp more fully the symbols of the intellectual life, to respond to these symbols more rationally, and, when confronted with an idea, to be less disturbed by self-centered affect. Despite these gains, they still experienced anxiety about taking exams, writing papers, and doing homework. But whatever their worries over particular assignments, most of these women nonetheless had confidence in their own abilities. For instance, though three in five of the married women who were enrolled in degree or certificate programs said that exams were a source of pressure, only one in four experienced anxiety because of inadequate study skills and one-third said that their lack of reading concentration, comprehension, or recall posed difficulties.

The enthusiasm of these women for ideas and learning is hard to match, even among professional scholars and scientists. As was pointed out in the previous chapter, an interest in learning and the desire to achieve independence and a sense of identity were their two most common objectives in coming to a continuing education program. Preparation for a job, or for a better job, was the third most common objective. In choosing their particular fields of study, three in four said that intrinsic interest was a very important factor; only one in four said that job opportunities in the field were very important. Excitement over learning and the desire to express one's capacities in a remunerative job do not, of course, exclude each other. It is possible that these women downplay jobs because they are unsure about being able to get them, given the present market and the limited opportunities for women, particularly middle-aged women. In this respect, they may resemble poor young people going to college during the depression years of the 1930s, who were caught up in the excitement of learning but did not expect their education to eventuate in high-level academic and professional jobs. We may surmise, following Valerie Oppenheimer's lead [1970], that as more jobs open up to women, more women will desire them.

Involvement with ideas was not, of course, the only reason for excitement over the return to school. There were other gratifications, two of which stand out. First of all, school provided an opportunity for new kinds of close associations with other people. Mostly these were with other women, but the interviewees who came in contact with men in their classes also mentioned their associations with them. Discussing ideas from their courses outside of the classroom, they find their own interests and abilities confirmed through seeing similar tendencies and capacities in other women and in men. They have opportunities for interactions different from those which might have developed in the neighborhood or on the park benches while babysitting. Some interviewees who had not had opportunities for getting together informally with other students complained about this lack. What happens in continuing education programs is what has been happening throughout the women's movement: women getting together, raising their consciousness, gaining strength and enjoyment from each other, developing a previously denied sense of what it can mean to be a woman. In addition they experience the shared sense of the community of scholars and ideas.

Second, as these women students looked forward to the practical applications of what they were learning, their strong orientation toward helping other people was evident. One in three of the married women said they would like ultimately to have jobs in counseling, social work, teaching, and similar helping professions. Another 13 percent wanted jobs in the arts or in writing and editing. Only 7 percent had their eye on upper-level business positions. These preferences may be a function of prior socialization and a reflection of continuing patterns in the labor market for women. As opportunities widen, the distribution of occupational choices may well change.

But this interest and pleasure in helping other people may also signify that, as they enter the world of work in larger numbers, women will be able—more fully than is the case in more male-dominated days—to relate ideas to the lives of people, to be concerned with the meaning of ideas in relation to feeling, and to consider their utility for the enlargement of feelings. Even in scientific endeavors, the more contextual and less abstract ways of thinking exhibited by many women may lead to theories that are more complex in their ideational content, experimental reach, experiential reference, and applicability. To make such a statement is not to place a special burden on women or to engage in one more bit of sex-typing, however generous; rather, it is to anticipate the invigoration that commonly takes place when previously excluded groups are allowed to join the established ones. The strong emphasis that these women in continuing education place on the intrinsic worth of ideas and on self-development is worth noting: Their values may prove to be a corrective to the overly pragmatic view with which education is frequently viewed in American society.

What Makes the Return to Education Possible?

Married women in continuing education programs may be a distinctive group. In the interviews, both the women and their husbands and children stressed their sense of purpose, energy, and determination. Described as "dynamos," they took pride in their perseverance and said that practically nothing could stop them in their pursuit of an education. It may be that, compared with other women, the women in our sample were more self-propelled, less passive, better able to get what they wanted. This characterization must, however, be qualified to some extent: Many interviewees hesitated a long time before enrolling in a continuing education program. One-third deliberated for up to six months before enrolling, and almost as many deliberated for six months to a year. The encouragement of counselors and other supportive people at the time when the decision to enroll was made and during the early stages of the return to education turned out to be crucial in the view of most interviewees. The more personal the counseling, whether individual or group, the more effective it was. Interviewees also remarked frequently that a talk by the director of the continuing education program was a precipitating event in their decision to enroll. Indeed, it is striking how important the directors of CEW programs were. Reference to them was made repeatedly in the interviews. Apparently the presence of a powerful model—a woman of great intelligence, accomplishment, and charismatic appeal—gives other women courage to develop their own capacities. Other inducements to enrollment were word-of-mouth reports and the presence of a program near enough to the home.

On the other side, funding the return to education can be a problem; only a third said that costs had not been an obstacle to their participation in the program. Our interviewees told us that, in allocations of money, the children's schooling (particularly college) had priority over the wife's education. Some women felt guilty even when there was little need for tight budgeting. Considering that our respondents were relatively well-off financially, funding may be an even bigger problem for most women than appears from our data. Consistent with their altruistic and outgoing orientation, many of our respondents were concerned about women less fortunate than they and urged that the program be made available to people from less educationally and financially advantaged social and racial/ethnic groups as well as to younger women and to men.

Since nearly two-thirds of the married women students had children under thirteen years old, fear of the "empty nest" was not a primary factor in the decision to return to school. For older women, however, the waning of domestic responsibilities and the anticipation of many vigorous years ahead was a strong incentive. The husbands of many of these women were especially encouraging of their return to school at that stage in life. But for both younger and older women, domestic life alone was not fulfilling.

The Husbands' Attitudes: Perception and Reality

As was mentioned in Chapter 4, most participants in CEW programs felt their husbands were supportive of their decision to return to school: 62 percent of the women characterized their husbands as very supportive, and an additional 20 percent found them somewhat supportive. (About one-tenth said their husbands were neutral, and only 5 percent said their husbands were not supportive.) Of students with supportive husbands, 42 percent reported that marital relations had improved and that they enjoyed greater rapport with their spouses as a result of participating in the program; only one in five of the women with nonsupportive husbands reported this effect.

Almost all students who described their marriages as happy also described their husbands as supportive. But only about half of those who described their marriages as unhappy said their husbands were supportive. Similarly the woman who rated herself high on success as a wife was more likely to characterize her husband as supportive than was the woman who gave herself an average or low ranking on this trait. One wonders whether the success as a wife facilitated support or whether husband's support augmented the sense of success. Most likely it is a combination of both.

In their responses to the questionnaire, the husbands usually confirmed what their wives had told us. For instance, with respect to demographic factors, the husband and wife agreed on the husband's age, education, and occupation. The only discrepancy concerned income. Fewer women reported high incomes and more women reported low incomes for their husbands than the husbands reported for themselves: 37 percent of the husbands compared to 28 percent of the wives said that his income was $30,000 or more. Only 10 percent of men and 12 percent of women said that the husband's income was less than $10,000. (This skewing is attributable to the sample's having been drawn largely from private selective institutions that serve a high-income population.)

Confirming the women's perception, husbands were overwhelmingly supportive of the return to school: 88 percent said that they agreed with their wives' decision to participate in the continuing education program when they *first* learned about it. By the time they responded to the questionnaire, only 4 percent of the husbands felt worse about the decision. The rest still supported it, and nearly one in four felt even better about it. In one extreme case, even the ex-husband of an interviewee was highly supportive of his former wife's CEW participation; his new wife and his mother babysat so that she could attend classes. While motives may have been mixed, the case dramatizes a more pervasive trend. When asked which persons were most supportive of their decision to return to school, the women we interviewed mentioned husbands first—ahead of women friends and children. Parents, siblings, and neighbors were far down on the list. Husbands also were by far the most frequent major source of financing the return to education, listed by 69 percent of the women. (But jobs, investments, savings, and loans were also named as major sources. It seems that many women must make an extra effort if they wish to continue their education.)

The husbands were supportive not only of their own wives' return to school but also of women's aspirations in general, strongly advocating the need for equality in economic and other spheres. They appreciated the women's liberation movement though they often registered objection to some of its tactics: 64 percent of the husbands said they approved of the women's movement; one in three had mixed feelings.

The husband tended to give the same reasons for the wife's return to education as she herself did, stressing her desire for personal growth and her interest in learning as the primary objectives. The husbands recognized, however, that their wives were going back to school not only for the sake of self-development and learning but also because of career aspirations. Three-fourths of the wives said that having a career in addition to being a wife and mother was important for their self-fulfillment. Nearly as many husbands said that a career was essential or very important to their wives. Husbands and wives also tended to agree on the appropriate age of the child before the mother returns to school or work. Half of the husbands and slightly more than half of the wives said that a return to work or school when the children are six years or younger is appropriate. Most of the remainder thought the children should be older. The husbands' supportiveness of their school-going and working wives are often accompanied by a high estimate of their wives' abilities as homemakers, wives, and mothers. The wives themselves had good opinions of themselves in these roles, but their husbands thought even better of them: 61 percent of the married women thought of themselves as above-average mothers, 77 percent of the husbands thought so. Fifty-five percent considered themselves above average in homemaking ability, 63 percent of the husbands thought so. Two-thirds of the wives thought of themselves as above-average wives, and an equal proportion of the husbands thought so too.

In considering this generally favorable picture of husband-wife relationships, one should bear in mind that it may in part be due to the special nature of our sample. Our sample of husbands and wives was drawn from intact families. That tensions exist elsewhere is indicated by, for instance, the report of 31 percent of the divorced, separated, or widowed respondents that the women's movement had threatened or contributed to the dissolution of their marriages. Moreover, we do not know what the situation is in families where the woman does not return to school; it seems likely that many women in that group have husbands whose lack of support for their interests and aspirations precludes their return to education.

The supportiveness of the husbands reflects a variety of motivations.

During the interviews, a number of husbands reiterated that if their wives were happy, they too would be happy. In some cases, this may be interpreted to mean that an unhappy woman is a bother to have around the house and her return to school is a lesser evil; in short, the husband's supportiveness springs from relatively selfish considerations. In other cases, this attitude indicates a more altruistic and empathetic concern that the wife be given an opportunity to develop her own potential. When we asked them whether their wife's seeking further schooling had their consent, some husbands even rejected the question. They felt that their wives were individuals and thus had the right to make their own decisions. Many husbands saw in their wives' working an opportunity for a better life for themselves. They anticipated a lessening of financial burdens and greater financial security as a result of their wives' educational or occupational plans, or they remarked on the possibility of taking time out for their own personal development. Some anticipated a reversal of traditional roles for considerable amounts of time, during which they would turn to pursuits important to them, such as sculpting and writing, while the wife would be the primary or only breadwinner.

Traditional attitudes also persist. Such phrases as "*I* will let her" or "*I* will not let her" still cropped up in the replies of some husbands. That the husband should be the sole breadwinner was maintained by 45 percent of the husbands. The rest believed that the responsibility should be shared by husband and wife—a remarkably untraditional attitude. No husband thought that the wife alone should be the wage-earner. Other studies indicate that many men cling to their traditional role as breadwinner [Katz, 1974]. In several repeated surveys of college students, males tended to say they would be willing to spend as much time in the rearing of their children as their future wives, but many were not as ready to share the task of financial support with her. This attitude is the more remarkable when one considers that the male students also thought a career important to a woman's sense of self-fulfillment. It seems that being the breadwinner is still an important ingredient in the self-esteem of many men.

The threat to men's self-esteem, as women enter the world of work in larger numbers, may at times have been symbolically expressed when the interviewed husbands registered objections to women taking on hard physical jobs, such as firefighting or coal mining. At least some of the husbands showed other signs of ambivalence. Though the interviewed women overwhelmingly described their husbands as supportive of their return to school, they also described occasions in which that support was half-hearted, as when the husband arranged a social engagement or a leisure activity that conflicted with the wife's school obligations or raised an eyebrow when she left house guests at the breakfast table in order to go to a class, or more important, made it clear that he expected no disturbance of the routines of the household because of the wife's schooling. On one occasion, when husband and wife were interviewed together, the husband remarked that he had picked strawberries to finance his education, and the wife replied—almost inaudibly—to the implied expectation that she felt her many years of domestic work had earned her the right to spend money now on her education.

Sometimes one got the impression that the husband was saying that his wife's activities were fine as long as they did not interfere with his life. In subtler forms this attitude may be very frequent. Men have suddenly been faced with changes in their role for which education has only partially prepared them. So they may be thinking and acting in contrary ways simultaneously. One man I interviewed said, "I married one woman, and now I have another." I asked him whom he preferred. He said, "the present one." But he, as well as other husbands, may also have been hankering for the more traditional woman his wife once was. Sometimes the pressures were more crude. One husband, a lawyer, was so hostile towards his wife's being in law school that she dropped out and started in the Attorney Assistant program, of which he approved. Another husband exerted pressures on his wife which contributed to her decision to drop out of a Ph.D. program in order to "stay married"; he encouraged her getting a master's degree, however. We do not know to what extent the supportiveness of the husband as reported by the women in our sample was on his own terms, thus interfering with the independence and identity his wife sought.

At the same time it is hard to disentangle the true attitudes of the husbands from the perceptions of their wives. Some studies [Steinmann and Fox, 1966] suggest that women tend to ascribe to their husbands more traditional concepts of women's roles than their husbands actually hold. Women's socializaton into the domestic role has a long history, particularly in the middle class. The women in our sample had spent many long years being wives and mothers, so it is not surprising that some experienced some difficulty in adapting to nondomestic roles. Some interviewees felt uncomfortable over time spent on school and home-work, time that seemed to be taken away from the family and from household tasks. One woman expressed guilt over neglecting the starching and ironing of her children's shirts. Another woman worried that her middle daughter might suffer because she (the mother) no longer had the time to make dresses with her and for her as she had done for her older daughter. Other interviewees said that they studied at hours which would least interfere with the family: when everyone else had gone to bed, for example. Many of these women were trying to do everything at once and became anxious if they could not. When asked what aspect of their school work created special anxieties, by far the most often-mentioned problem was conflicting demands on time. As we have already seen, 70 percent listed that as a source of pressure. Even as one must admire the stamina and energy of these women, one wonders whether so much sacrifice is really necessary, and whether guilt does not add strain and interfere with finding relief. For instance, when interviewees complained about lack of desk and other space to study, the idea suggested itself that, if guilt were less, such facilities might more easily be found.

What help with domestic tasks did these married women students get from their husbands? Nearly half of the husbands interviewed reported that they have taken on more chores around the house, very willingly. Questionnaire responses gave some sense of the current division of labor in the household: 56 percent of the husbands never washed clothes, but 44 percent always did the gardening and yard work. About two-thirds sometimes cared for or supervised the children, did the grocery shopping, cooked, washed dishes, and cleaned the house. With the mother's return to school, the children were more fully enlisted in domestic work, and their parents told us in the interviews that these tasks were good for them in that they increased the children's independence. (If more mothers realized such gains, their sense of guilt over not spending more time with the children might be alleviated.)

Whatever the additional efforts required of them, the husbands seemed pleased with the domestic results of their wives' return to school. They said that the quality of the interaction around the dinner table or in joint family activities was much higher than previously, when a sort of indifferent loafing might have characterized such occasions. They found their wives more interesting, learned a lot from their reports of studies and work activities, and enjoyed their company more, in part because of their more confident and assertive behavior. At times, stimulated by their wives, husbands joined in educational activities, and the couple took courses together. Fifty-eight percent of the husbands believed that the educational and occupational activities of their wives would make their marriage a better partnership, and 74 percent looked forward to benefiting from the wife's experience and to learning through her. One-third of both husbands and wives asserted that the wife's participation in a continuing education program had brought the family closer together, that they talked things over more. One in three husbands also said that the marriage had improved, and about the same proportion of wives agreed. As one interviewed woman put it, she no longer exerted pressure on her husband for vicarious achievement, prestige, and excitement in life. Only 4 percent of the husbands said that the marriage had suffered; 10 percent of the wives and 12 percent of the husbands reported tensions and strains in their relationship as a result of the wife's participation in a continuing education program.

Though husbands and wives both tended to say that the effects of returning to school had been beneficial to their marriages, our data also indicate that a particular husband and wife often did not hold the same views. One partner was more inclined than the other to see the situation as favorable. Here then is another piece of evidence of the discrepancies characterizing many marriages.

Effects on the Children

Only 1 percent of the men and 4 percent of the women thought that the wife's participating in a continuing education program has had bad effects on the children. On the other hand, 31 percent of the husbands reported positive effects on the children, and 54 percent of the wives said that their children's respect and regard for them had increased.

Some of the women interviewed said that their return to school was in part motivated by the desire to present their children with a model of the importance of school and learning. Even when this was not a primary intent, the children's performance and interest in school had considerably advanced. Children would do their homework alongside mother, mother and child would discuss a book they had both read in school, and so forth.

Some children told us that when their mother returned to school, they thought it somewhat odd that she would be a student at so advanced an age. But now they were proud of it and even bragged about it to their friends, particularly if mother was doing well in school or had received some other form of recognition. All the children questioned thought their mother was a good student; 95 percent believed that she would finish her program.

The children confirmed what we had heard from their parents, describing themselves as having become more independent, participating more in household tasks, and otherwise learning to care for themselves and others. They did not idealize domestic chores or regard them as fun, but they were willing to do them if it helped mother to pursue her objectives more successfully. The mother's going to school typically meant more vigorous and entertaining talk at home, as well as access to previously unavailable experiences that had now been opened up because of the woman's greater acquaintance with interesting places to go or because more interesting people, her new friends, now visited the home.

At times children said they had been apprehensive when mother first started in the program. A seventeen-year-old daughter was "afraid things might fall apart at home." An eleven-year-old son wondered when his mother would be at home and whether he would have to do more work around the house. A twelve-year-old girl "thought we'd go broke." But, as with the husbands, more children came to approve of their mother's return to school after they had experienced it for a while: 47 percent said they were glad when they first heard about her decision to enroll; 74 percent were glad at the time of the interview. (Fifteen percent were indifferent, 7 percent ambivalent, and 4 percent disapproving.)

Occasionally, mother's being in school made for friction. At exam time, one might have to tiptoe around and even accept her being irritable. At other times, when she studied, mother might not be as accessible as she once had been. Many children expressed a desire for mother to be at home when they returned from school. Some children expressed a certain longing for more time with mother. One boy felt envious because his mother did not do at home the interesting things she did with the students she was teaching at her school. Another boy expressed ambivalence, saying that women should have access to any occupation, provided that they have the qualifications to do the things "they are screaming about." We would need more data to understand the sources of this boy's reactions. Had he more or less consciously identified with his father, who in this case was not too happy about his wife's return to education? Was he too dependent on his mother? Was he, like other males in our culture, not readily able to identify with a woman's aspirations?

One daughter, supportive of her mother's return to school, told us that women cannot be expected just to scrub floors, vacuum, and clean the house. Her mother's action seemed to encourage her own development. She said she had an opportunity for more independence because her mother was doing less for her; she even added, bravely, that she was getting experience for the time when she would be a mother herself and would need to take care of things.

Children's attitudes are, of course, determined by a web of circumstances, including the often traditional and stereotypical attitudes of people in one's social network. No clear ideological guidelines exist as to what the appropriate roles are for wife and husband, mother and child. Mothers may be hesitant in their new roles and convey that uncertainty to their children. Fathers may be ambivalent. Beneath the hesitancy and ambivalence revolving around the mother's working or going to school are the perennial problems created by children's dependency, by the emotional demands they make upon their parents, and by the guilts, conflicts, and needs that parents have vis-a-vis their children. The women in our sample are pioneers of a life style that has not yet been fully charted. The children we interviewed seemed to point to a different future, too. Three in five said they would live their life differently than their mothers: They would go to school earlier, have fewer children, time them differently, or marry later or not at all. Their mothers were often stuck with the consequences of a life plan that no longer fit with their beliefs; hence there was some confusion and even suffering. Yet the rewards were many. As one woman put it, she now much more enjoyed the company of other women and she enjoyed men more, because she no longer felt resentful of being kept down. She now had a sense of equality; having learned to be more just to herself, she could be more just to men.

Separated and Divorced Women Students

What about those women who were wholly without the support of marital partners? In our sample of participants, 12 percent were divorced, and 3 percent were separated from their husbands. About a third of this group singled out marital problems as a major catalyst in their going back to school. Like their married peers, they too were strongly oriented toward becoming more educated and achieving independence and identity. But, not surprisingly, job preparation was a more salient objective for them than for the married students. To be in school, they had to overcome more obstacles than the absence of a supportive husband; money was a particular problem. Many more of the divorced women than the married ones were employed, and more of them worked full-time.

Yet, despite the failure of their marriages, the divorced and separated women seemed to have high self-esteem. They felt that their self-confidence, realistic self-assessment, and intelligence all contributed to their progress in the program, and they ascribed these qualities to themselves much more frequently than did the married students. They also were more inclined to rate themselves high on leadership ability, independence, and even cheerfulness. One wonders whether the separation or divorce stimulated these women to develop these capacities more strongly or whether their greater self-confidence and independence made it easier for them to forge ahead on their own. Probably the answer is different for different people.

Speaking of the effects that her return to school had on her children, the divorced or separated woman tended to be as positive as her married peer. She too described her family as closer and more self-reliant, and the children as having a higher regard for her as a result of the program. In spite of her greater burdens, the divorced or separated woman was less apt to report anxiety over taking exams, writing papers, or speaking in class than was the married woman. But it should also be emphasized that these apparently sturdy women often cited the encouragement of others as a very important factor in their coming to the program: Nearly half of them mentioned such encouragement as a catalyst, compared with only 28 percent of the married students. This finding underscores the point made earlier about the emotional facilitation that is often required in the return to education.

Summary

In summary, the major findings are:

- Emotionally and financially, husbands were strongly supportive of their wives' returning to school, though their support also showed ambivalence.
- Many wives and husbands reported that their marriages had improved. Practically no one reported that the marriage had suffered.
- Many wives and husbands reported that the family had drawn closer together and that the effects on the children were positive, including greater independence, responsibility, and interest in school. The children's respect for their mothers had increased.
- Nearly all married women students reported increased self-awareness, self-esteem, and greater happiness in their personal lives.

It seems clear that returning to education not only greatly enhances a woman's intellectual and personal well-being but also does not detract from her carrying out the domestic tasks traditionally assigned to her. In fact, many women seem to do better at them, perhaps because by giving attention to their own development they feel less strain and frustration.

The results of our study are corroborated by another recent study [Ballmer and Cozby, 1975], which showed that two-thirds of the women returning to education considered knowledge and self-improvement their primary objectives. In addition, the husbands and wives in their sample reported that their marriages, including sexual relations, had improved. Some husbands, however, were ambivalent about their wives' getting more education. Finally, Ballmer and Cozby found that the children benefited from the mother's educational involvement, showing increased appreciation for education and more willingness to accept responsibilities; sometimes, however, they resented the loss of mother's attention and time.

Allison Parelman [1974], in a study based on two of the fifteen programs that we studied, reports that husbands and children are generally supportive of the woman's return to school. But she too found ambivalence and was able to ascertain some of the conditions that are likely to encourage more full-hearted support:

1. The family will be more supportive if the marriage is already in some ways nontraditional in role assignments (e.g., housework, outside employment).
2. The more the husband agrees with his wife's decision, the more likely he is substantially to share in the household tasks.

3. The mother who is venturing out of the homemaking role for the first time will express more guilt feelings and be more accommodating to family needs and demands (e.g., housework) than the previously employed mother.

Parelman's findings are consistent with those reported by Lois Hoffman [1974] in her comprehensive review of research on the effects of maternal employment on the child. The child's attitudes are affected by, among other things, the meaning ascribed to maternal employment by the social network (father, peers, society) and by the mother's actual and perceived attitude toward working. The enthusiasm for school among the women in our sample seems to have been one factor favorably disposing the children toward their mother's new role.

Some Unanswered Questions

Though one might have expected to find that the married woman's return to school might result in many disruptions and tensions in family life, what we actually found was that husbands and children tended to be supportive of and satisfied with the arrangement. This is surprising when one considers that the women's movement has only recently gained momentum and that traditional social mores decree that wives and mothers devote themselves to the home. That there was relatively little strain as the woman moved into her new role indicates that there is a greater readiness to accept new arrangements than has previously been recognized. In light of our results, it now seems desirable to study a sample, as closely matched as possible to the sample in this study, of the families of women who do not return to school in order to learn what relations obtain in such families and what self-concepts these women have. Such a study might reveal the conditions under which traditional family patterns impose undue strains upon women and their families.

It also seems desirable to get more evidence about the personal characteristics and environmental circumstances that account for the mature woman's return to education. At first glance, it might be supposed that the women we studied are unusually energetic and independent people or perhaps simply people with a special inclination toward education. Our data suggest a different picture: The return to school seems to have been strongly facilitated by the availability of a continuing education program, by the use of special means to bring it to the attention of women in the community, and by counseling and other personal supports to ease the transition. Still, we need more information—and more programs—to answer such questions as how many women (with what social and psychological characteristics) would avail themselves of properly devised continuing education programs.

While we were able to determine the degree of family acceptance and some of the outcomes of the married woman's return to school, we have insufficient information about the processes by which the realignment took place. It would be helpful to learn more about how family members redefine their roles and attitudes and discover new ways of relating to each other. For instance, our study suggests that some women students, guilty about their return to school, take upon themselves more of the domestic burden than is absolutely necessary and that husbands and children react to their uncertainty by making heavier demands. In other families the husband's sense of self undergoes a sudden and painful diminution, or the children feel insecure. On the positive side, the mother's return to school sets the stage for an increase in purposive activities for each member of the family and for more mutually respectful and enjoyable relations between husband and wife. These and other processes deserve attention. Such a study would provide valuable guidelines for families struggling through transitional periods and useful information for continuing education program counselors. Even our present knowledge suggests that, to alleviate concerns and assure greater cooperation and understanding, more opportunities should be provided for children and husbands to discuss their feelings about the woman's return to school.

It also seems highly desirable to revisit some of or all the families in our sample some years hence to determine the long-range impact of the woman's return to school. One remarkable aspect of the present study is that it has allowed us to watch part of a social revolution in progress. The attitudes of and the arrangements between men and women are in flux. It seems likely that the husband's self-concept, his relations with his wife, and his work and leisure behavior will change even more profoundly. The family—its size, roles, relations, and activities—has entered a stage of accelerated evolution. If we are to understand and to guide these processes, we need continuing studies.

**Part III
What the Future Holds**

Women's Continuing Education: Whither Bound?

Jessie Bernard

This book began with a historical survey of the women's continuing education movement over the last fifteen years. At this point a few comments on possible trends in the next fifteen years may be appropriate. These trends will be determined by both the "demand" for continuing education made by women and the "supply" of such services that institutions are willing and able to provide. The discussion here is admittedly speculative, but the subject is worth at least a passing bow.

The Future "Demand" and "Supply"

At least three demographic factors will affect the "demand" for women's continuing education in the next decade and a half: marriage and fertility rates, a growing appetite for education among women, and trends in the participation of women in the labor force.

Since women's continuing education programs are designed primarily for women who wish to return to school after time out for marriage and motherhood, data on marriage and fertility are relevant in projecting trends for the future. It is noteworthy, therefore, that the demographic picture in the middle of the 1970s is very different from that of the early 1960s, when continuing education for women first burst upon the academic scene. In 1960–1962, for example, the first-marriage rate for women fourteen to forty-four years of age was 115 per thousand; in 1972–1974, it was down to 99. (The remarriage rate had increased from 133 to 164 in the same period; it may now be decreasing). More to the point, perhaps, is that age at first marriage has risen from 20.3 in 1960 to 21.1 in 1974. In the words of Paul Glick:

By the mid-1950s, a relatively familistic period had arrived. Couples were entering marriage at the youngest ages on record, and all but four percent of those at the height of the childbearing period eventually married. Moreover, the baby boom that had started with the return of World War II service men reached a plateau in the mid-1950s and did not diminish significantly until after 1960. By that time, the rate of entering first marriage had already been falling. . . . By the late 1960s and early 1970s, the familistic style of life seemed to be on the wane. . . . The marriage rate among single persons under 45 years old was as low as it had been at the end of the Depression. Last year, the average age at marriage was close to a year higher than it had been in the mid-1950s, and the proportion of

109

women who remained single until they were 20 to 24 years old had increased by one-third since 1960 [Glick, 1975, p. 16].[a]

Along with older age at first marriage and lower marriage rate has gone the almost spectacular decline in fertility rates. Total fertility peaked in 1957 at 3.8 children; it has now fallen to less than 2.0.[1] As a concomitant of delayed marriage, since 1968 the median age at the birth of the first child has risen from 21.8 in 1960 to 22.1 today.

It was the demographic situation in the early 1960s which produced the women—now in their mid-thirties—who currently participate in continuing education programs. It is those women who, fifteen to twenty years ago, were marrying in such large numbers and having so many babies at such an early age that now constitute a large part of the clientele for continuing education. Will their younger sisters follow in their footsteps? Will their lower marriage and fertility rates make a difference? Not necessarily. For a fast-growing "appetite" for education seems to characterize women of all ages today.

This appetite for education among both college-age and adult women is manifested in increased school and college enrollments of all ages from sixteen to thirty-four. Indeed, the increase in college enrollment has been spectacular: "Almost three times as many women were enrolled in college in 1972 as in 1960 (3.5 million versus 1.2 million), and the college enrollment rate ... more than doubled for women in their twenties during those twelve years" [Glick, 1975, p. 17]. More to the point, an increasing number of young *married* women, ages twenty-two to twenty-four, were enrolled in college (199,000 in 1973 as compared with 69,000 in 1965) and half (50.8 percent) were enrolled full-time.

Looking at college enrollments by marital status and age, we find that the number of single women ages eighteen to twenty-one —undergraduates, that is—seems no longer to be increasing; the number of older single women—ages twenty-two to twenty-four—continues to increase, though moderately. But the picture for married women is somewhat different and varies with age. As a concomitant of the current tendency for young women to delay marriage, the number of married women ages eighteen to twenty-one enrolled in college has begun to decline. But the number of married women twenty-two to twenty-four years of age has begun to rise fairly markedly. Apparently many women beyond the usual age at graduation (generally twenty-two) were not taking time out for marriage or for motherhood immediately after graduation; marriage was not making serious dislocations in their educational plans.[2]

If this trend toward continuing their education immediately after the bachelor's degree should prove persistent, it might mean fewer women would need the kind of continuing education programs designed for women who have dropped out. If, however, these young women are merely delaying the time when they drop out to have children, the demand will merely be postponed for them, and they will be slightly older when they return.

Since continuing education programs are designed in large part to help adult women prepare for participation in the labor force, the increase in that participation—among women in general but especially among mothers—is also relevant for the future. Between 1960 and 1974, the proportion of mothers of preschool children who were in the labor force rose from 18.6 percent to 34.4 percent; and of mothers of school-age children, but not of preschoolers, the proportion rose from 39 percent to 51.2 percent. The impact that current trends in the economy may have on these increases in participation is dealt with below.

These, then, are some of the straws that show which way the wind is blowing: The number of women who are not marrying or who are delaying marriage is increasing; the number of children they are having or want to have is declining; more of those who do marry are remaining in school, half of them full-time; and more of those with children have been entering the labor force.

On the supply side of the equation, data on trends over the past decade and a half are not as readily available. It would be useful to know the number of institutions which have offered continuing education programs, as well as the kinds of programs offered. Unfortunately neither kind of information exists.[3] It is, therefore, impossible to use the past growth in the supply of continuing education programs as a basis for projecting the future. No wonder that the several attempts to do so have ended in frustration [U.S. Department of Labor, 1974, p. 1; Mattfeld, quoted by Cless, this book, p. 00].

Although it is not possible to offer clear-cut numerical data on the past growth of the continuing education movement, still, for whatever it may be worth, an attempt is made here. First, between the number of services initially offered by the institutions included in the present study and the number offered by them at the present time, the increase has been 100 percent—from 29 to 58. On a wider scale, the picture is somewhat different. Figure 6-1 charts what the Women's Bureau calls, without definition, "offerings."

So much, then, for the trends relevant to the future of women's continuing education. Unfortunately one cannot simply add up two sets of trends and divide by two to locate the probable direction they indicate. Instead three possible "scenarios" are discussed here.

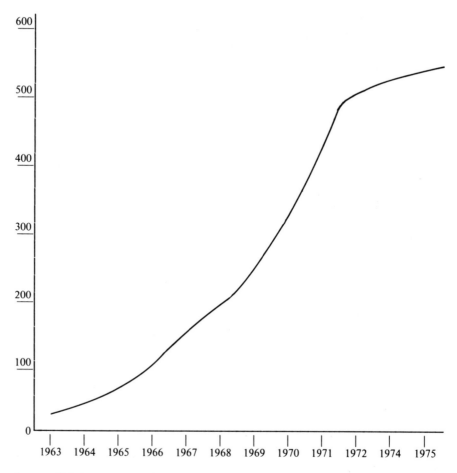

Source: U.S. Department of Labor, Employment Standards Administration, Women's Bureau. *Continuing Education for Women: Current Developments.* Washington, D.C.: Government Printing Office, 1974, p. 2. The data on which this figure is based are admittedly rough. The 1963 figure is based on a "cursory review" and the 1974 figure is "estimated to exceed 500."

Figure 6–1. Women's Continuing Education Offerings, 1963–1974.

Three Scenarios

On the basis of the sets of trends just discussed, three possible futures suggest themselves: (1) a continuation of the past rise; (2) a tapering-off and, ultimately, a flattening of the curve at some future date, in accordance with the usual growth curve; and (3) a decline.

Scenario 1: A "Bullish" Future

The Women's Bureau—on the basis of the needs of women themselves, on one hand, and the needs of the economy, on the other—is "bullish" about women's continuing education programs:

There is little doubt that much more expansion of programs must occur before the educational needs of mature women approach fulfillment. So long as large numbers of educational institutions fail to consider continuing education programs for women as potentially part of their standard educational offerings, a glaring gap will remain between demand (expressed or unexpressed) and response. . . .

The value of these programs and courses to other groups in our society has also become evident as the movement has developed. Our expanding economy has made it essential for more adult women to participate in the work force. This, in turn, has increased the interest of employees and educators in establishing courses and services which would prepare women for entry or re-entry into employment. . . .

Further development of continuing education for women is therefore a necessity for the attainment of goals desired by women individually and society at large. [U.S. Department of Labor, 1974, pp. 11–12]

The data about college enrollments, reviewed earlier, seem to support the point of view that the future of continuing education programs is promising. I shall comment presently on both grounds for optimism offered.[4]

Scenario 2: A Diffusion Model

A second scenario posits a leveling-off when all the women with an appetite for education have been reached, and all the schools willing or able to supply courses have responded. I have looked at sex-role change as an example of the standard growth curve as applied to cultural diffusion; the increase in the demand by women and in the supply of offerings may follow such a curve, conceived of as either growth or diffusion [Bernard, 1975].

According to one conceptualization, diffusion can be viewed in terms of the readiness of different components of a population to accept the trait being diffused. Thus, individuals can be categorized—according to when in the course of events they accept a change—as: innovators, early adopters, early majority, late majority, and laggards. Institutions may also be categorized in these terms. In the present context, the initial breakthrough by the institutional innovators—Radcliffe, Minnesota, Sarah Lawrence—occurred in the early 1960s; the laggards—some of the prestigious universities—may hold out for a longer time.

As applied to women, the innovators tend to be exceptional women who have the stamina and ability to pioneer. But, as Felice Schwartz reminds us, they constitute only the "small percentage of women who are prepared to make a full-time, life-time commitment to work. The real needs of the vast majority of women must also be considered" [1973, p. 180]. Most women are not superstars who can manage somehow or other to make a career for themselves; rather, "the majority of women want to combine family and work and . . . require part-time" commitments, whether it be to work or to study [Schwartz, 1973, p. 181]. They are the early and late majority who flock to continuing education programs once the forest of institutional obstacles has been removed and the road cleared. And then, of course, there are the women who simply have no wish to continue their education, no matter how auspicious conditions may be. If women's continuing education follows this diffusion scenario, the upward trend may taper off, perhaps in the 1980s. By that time the movement may have attracted all the women who want or need such programs, and their needs may have been responded to by all the schools that are likely ever to accept it.

Scenario 3: Decline

A third possibility is that offerings will not sustain themselves, as in the diffusion model, but will actually begin to decline. This possibility augurs either a positive or a negative consequence so far as women are concerned. If such a decline came about because all schools accommodated their programs for what is now coming to be called recurrent education—with such features as flexibility, part-time study, greater accessibility, and counseling[5]—or adopted these features and made such a program available to anyone who wanted it, thus obviating the need for special programs for adult women, that would be a plus, for women as well as for others. And there do seem to be adumbrations of such a trend, however faint.[6] If it continues, Ms. Cless's prescient comment in Chapter 1 of this book, "women's continuing education may be victorious . . . even if unsung," will indeed become a reality. For, as she notes: "Almost every innovation [suggested by the advocates of nontraditional education] has been a part of women's continuing education programs for ten to fifteen years." If new patterns of thinking about education as a recurring life-long enterprise for everyone take hold, perhaps women's continuing education programs can enjoy the satisfaction of having accomplished their mission, and the shop can be closed.

Even if the millenium of recurrent education for everyone does not come to pass, certain demographic changes might produce new life schedules for women that would lessen the need for special offerings in continuing education.[7] For example, if many women remained single, or married but had no children, they would not need the continuing education programs designed for women with family responsibilities. Or if young women delayed marriage and childbearing until they completed their education and professional training and established a toehold in their professions without taking time out, this would also reduce the need for special programs, especially if they retained continuity with their professions, as they are now urged to do, when they take time out for children.[8] Declines in offerings due to such changes either in institutions or in women would not result in or reflect deprivations for women. A decline might, in such cases, represent an advance.

On the other hand, a decline might, in fact, reflect adverse conditions: a long recession, for example.

The Impact of a Faltering Economy

The third demographic trend referred to earlier—the increased participation of women in the labor force, especially of mothers—has a very direct bearing on the future of women's continuing education. Women's continuing education programs serve a diversified clientele, including women who wish to prepare for more skilled jobs as well as women who wish to pursue professional careers. Both jobs and careers are vulnerable to the vicissitudes of the labor market.

In Chapter 1, Ms. Cless reminds us that the inception of the movement for women's continuing education in the 1960s came at a time of great economic and educational expansion. The ambience of the post-Sputnik years was one that fostered the mind-salvaging work the movement was designed to do. Many kinds of trained people were in short supply: There were not enough teachers for all those postwar babies; there were not enough engineers, doctors, or technicians. Talk of "brain gain" and "brain drain" was common, as scientists from other countries came to supply deficits.[9] Women's continuing education was easy to "sell."

The 1970s present a somewhat different economic—as well as demographic—picture. The expansionist mood in academia has withered, and the argument that we need all the brains we can train is less convincing than it once was. Why should we be making such an effort to preserve or inculcate skills for a job market that may not be there?

Hilda Kahne, for example, notes that in the coming decade "demand for new teachers will not increase so rapidly as the supply of potential teachers. . . . If past trends continue, the National Science Foundation anticipates an oversupply of about 40,000 . . . science and engineering doctorates in 1980" [1973, pp. 161, 162]. She concludes that "the data are a cause for sober concern and reflection about policies and priorities with respect to educational training and career directions" [1973, p. 162]. In this line of thought she is joined by Dorothy Zinberg, who also speaks of the danger of too great expectations:

In the next decade, which might now be called a "Climate of Great Expectations," we may unwittingly be preparing many gifted young women for "Great Disappointments," if we do not thoroughly understand the kinds of personal dilemmas they still face, and through this provide structural changes that will make it possible for them to follow careers if they choose to do so [Zinberg, 1973, p. 132].[10]

And Matina Horner echoes the same theme: "One concern is how to resolve the potential conflict between the new expectations . . . and the realities of a newly constrained and suffering economy and scarce resources" [1974, p. 4].

Nor is such concern restricted to women. James O'Toole, in a sobering article on the world of work, foresees a "reserve army of the underemployed" as more and more young people seek the education to qualify for interesting jobs while the actual supply of such jobs dries up. Women are among the most seriously affected:

Today . . . a growing number of women want and expect the same psychological and social rewards from work that men receive—a sense of identity, self-esteem, and mastery. . . . That they have largely been denied these satisfactions due to the maldistribution of good jobs has led to the most important and far-reaching social movement of the age. The desire for good jobs—not just any jobs—has become a hall-mark of the women's liberation movement. . . . The market has clearly failed to meet the underemployment problems of such groups as women, the disadvantaged, and subprofessionals. Although in one sense there is a general shortage of good jobs, the effects of underemployment are thus distributed differentially across the spectrum of workers, hitting hardest those with personal characteristics that have "low market value"—that is, blacks, women, those with little schooling, old people, young people, and even ugly people. These people do not have a share of good jobs proportionate to their share of human resources (in terms of talent, skills, intelligence, willingness to work, and so forth). [O'Toole, 1975, pp. 33, 63.]

And, finally, Janet Norwood [1975], of the Bureau of Labor Statistics, corroborates the same trends. The Bureau foresees that as early as 1985 the number of educated people will far exceed the number of available jobs calling for people with education.

The combination of a faltering economy and a lengthy decline in jobs calling for highly educated men and women might well produce a decline in both the "demand" and the "supply" side of the women's continuing education equation: a decline, that is, in both the number of educational offerings and the number of women seeking to take advantage of them.

Have We Oversold Careers For Women?

Mary Bunting tells us that "as long as able and responsible women wish to combine career and home responsibilities, institutions should schedule educational and job opportunities adapted to their needs" [1973, p. 211]. But what if, in light of the trends just sketched, the desire of women to combine career and home responsibilities subsides? What if we have oversold careers for women? These questions deserve our most thoughtful consideration.

The pessimistic pictures that some observers of the contemporary scene have drawn trouble me more than does the impact of a recession or lack of suitable jobs for the educated. Matina Horner, one of the most perceptive observers of the current scene, tells us, for example, of senior college women who are not yet psychologically together, who have the verbiage of the new ideology but not as yet an understanding of it, who are planning for neither marriage nor careers. They may talk a good liberation line but not yet have a gut-feeling for it [Horner, 1974, p. 5].[11] And Ms. Horner holds us at least partially to account: " . . . we haven't been terribly fair with our young people about all the realities, the cost-benefits of the new kind of life style they seek and value." Consequently, too many young women are expecting instant happiness because so little emphasis has been placed on the trade-offs involved in nontraditional roles and career orientations. Thus these women are unaware of the full implications of the choices they make. "In the long run that is what equality is all about: knowing what you are and being able to make a choice."

Women's Continuing Education and Mental Health

If women's continuing education were only a degree-granting or a professional or a vocational training program, the discouraging prospects for the job market might well produce a sharp decline in both offerings and students. But women's continuing education has other bows in its quiver, including not only the manifest function of education in and of itself but also the latent function of maintaining mental health.

To those in the monastic tradition of higher education, any noncognitive, nonintellectual function is anathema, secondary, or incidental at best, and preferably ignored. Still, in any overall assessment of continuing education, the mental-health aspect, even if it is viewed as serendipitous, cannot be discounted or negatively judged. For, on the basis of the data gathered by the present project as well as elsewhere, continuing education programs seem to have salutary effects on the mental health of participants.[12]

Elsewhere I have labeled the mental health of housewives as public health problem number one [Bernard, 1971, 1972]. A sizable research literature documents the mental-health hazards to which married women are subject [Gove, 1972]. Women's continuing education programs provide not only counseling, intellectual stimulation, support in the companionship of like-minded fellow students, and improved self-concepts, but also escape from the deteriorating effects of isolation. It is important to note that, on seven items in the present study that may be said to have mental-health implications, almost six times as many women on the average reported positive influences as reported negative ones. "No woman who has enjoyed the fruits of recurrent education can complain of being empty, frustrated, and alone" [Kline, 1973, p. 175].

Women's Continuing Education and E.R.A.

The rationale for maintaining programs for women (distinct from coeducational centers of continuing education) is still valid so long as there are separate and pressing requests by women, including those with little or no job skills but desirous of obtaining special assistance, counseling, and training prior to returning to mainstream activities. [U.S. Department of Labor, 1974, p. 12]

Will this rationale hold up under ERA? Although no one knows for sure yet what all the ramifications of the Equal Rights Amendment will be, still it is not too early to ask what effect, if any, it will have on educational programs designed primarily for women.

The question may be viewed from two angles. Women's continuing education programs may well be viewed as one method of overcoming discriminatory conditions in the present system. Esther M. Westervelt has summarized the institutional barriers and social constraints that, although not specifically intended to, have discriminatory consequences for women because of differences in the life schedules of men and of women. They include: admission rules dealing with age, rules with respect to part-time study, rules with respect to the transfer of credit, and practices with respect to financial aid [Westervelt, 1975, pp. 9–12, 17, 22]. Viewed from this angle, women's continuing education programs would not be interdicted by ERA.

Conversely, however, it could be argued that where there is a women's continuing education program—college and university courses offered at times and places to accommodate workers, for example—there must also be one for men. It might be argued that any program tailored to the needs of women—courses on "Single Women" or "Wives of Executives," for example—is forbidden if it is not equally available for men. Contrariwise, it will certainly be argued that all programs open to men must also be open to women.

I do not anticipate serious damage to programs for women from the argument that women's continuing education programs, or surrogates, be available to men. There is one possible exception. It has to do with courses which have consciousness-raising effects. Joseph Katz, in his perceptive and appreciative contribution to this book, notes that much of what happens in continuing education programs involves women developing a sense of sisterhood and identification with each other. The presence of men often precludes the benefits of such sisterhood.

This issue of separation or integration in education is one of the oldest we have had to face. Florence Howe hopes we will not fall into either of the two errors of the first century of women's education:

I hope we have learned to avoid both mistakes of the first century of education for women. I hope that we will go neither the route of total separation nor attempt total assimilation . . . . In this second century of women's education, perhaps women and men will study alone some of the time—to review their separate histories, to talk of their dreams and fears—and sometimes they will study together. [Howe, 1973, p. 127]

One argument in favor of permitting, even encouraging, men to participate in courses designed for women is the urgent need to get much of the research on which many of these courses are based into the mainstream of academic teaching and discussion. An impressive corpus of research in literature, criticism, history, economics, political science, sociology, and psychology has appeared in the last decade but as yet has not achieved the recognition it merits and must have to exert its salutary effect on these several disciplines as now taught. Encouraging men to register for such courses and male faculty to undertake to teach them would be one possible way to mainstream this important work.

New Models for a New World: Continuity Versus Recurrence

In 1971 I sketched the several options women had theoretically in planning their life schedules. They could plan their interruptions for childbearing early or late. But whichever they chose, the assumption was that interruption was inevitable. At the present time there is coming to be a decreased emphasis on continuity in either work or education. There is a greater emphasis on what is coming to be called recurrent education: alternating periods of work and education.

The concept of a career implies continuity. Interruptions for whatever reason are viewed as inimical to a career. They must be judiciously timed, of minimum duration, and, if possible, not total. In the case of women, interruptions for childbearing and childrearing have been viewed as all but disqualifying for a serious career.

But this concept of career is coming increasingly under challenge. Under the influence of this challenge I have recently been commenting on and, along with many others, propagating the idea of *flexitime* Bernard, [1972, 1975], one aspect of which takes the form of recurrent periods of education [Rehn, 1973, pp. 177–185]. The concept of flexitime, much elaborated in Europe and Japan, has only recently attracted attention in the United States. For the most part it refers to work: The general idea is that work should be organized so that individuals can be granted a certain degree of latitude in deciding the hours—even weeks, months, years—they will devote to work or other activities. These activities can include leisure or education or *childbearing and childrearing.* The concept is now being extended to education where it has been applied (especially to young people) with emphasis on the value of punctuating school experience with periods of work experience. But it is applicable over a lifetime.

The individual should be free to switch between periods of income-earning work, education, or training and leisure (including retirement) according to his (or her) own interests. There should also be many different and variable patterns of working time over the course of a year, a week or a day so that the individual can always find something that suits his (or her) preferences.

Of course, this freedom cannot be unlimited; the task is always to find the best compromise between individual wishes and the technical and economic exigencies which have led to existing rules and regulations whose role in promoting both economic efficiency and social protection should not be overlooked. But the time has come to move the point of compromise toward freedom by offering more flexibility whenever possible. [Rehn, 1973, p. 179]

The relevance of flexitime for women is clear. Constantina Safilios-Rothschild shows how it could help integrate work and family roles:

The concept of work continuity needs to be rethought. Is it really necessary and desirable that people have uninterrupted work records if they are to be considered good, serious, reliable and committed workers? Are people's "blind spots" in their work records not accounted for in terms of related work necessarily stigmata? Is taking time out to travel, to paint, to think and write, to have fun and enjoy life necessarily an indication of unreliability and lack of commitment? . . . Such structural flexibility in the occupational structure would tend to "normalize" work discontinuity and to lessen the strains on men and women with equal commitment to family and occupational roles. Thus, compromises in the performance of the occupational role could be avoided by temporarily withdrawing from the work force to attend to demanding family responsibilities, or to care for and enjoy a growing baby or to concentrate on a pet project, or to experience some desirable life experiences. The normalization of breaks in one's work records would render such temporary withdrawal from work only minor occupational setbacks rather than indications of failure and long-term handicaps. [Safilios-Rothschild, 1975, forthcoming]

And Gosta Rehn adds frosting to the cake by showing how flexitime could contribute to "solving the inflation-unemployment dilemma" by matching supply and demand in the labor market in part by promoting "voluntary variations in the supply of labor" and replacing "involuntary and destructive unemployment with agreeable leisure and useful studies" [1973, p. 178].

Women may have been leading the way in more ways than in continuing education alone. The wheel they invented is, indeed, being reinvented. The actual future of women's continuing education—continued growth, stabilization, or decline—will be the outcome of all the trends referred to here plus, no doubt, many more, interacting with one another either to augment or to cancel one another's impact. My personal view is that the concepts on which it is based are so obviously correct for this day and age, not only for women but for everyone, that whatever name it goes under—recurrent or continuing education—it has a guaranteed future and a clientele that will include both sexes.

Addendum

The discussion in the body of this chapter has had to do with innovations in traditional institutions. In the Women's Bureau's 1971 survey of offerings, all were in colleges, universities, or institutes of one kind or another. But this covers only one kind of women's continuing education, a kind that accepts traditional ideologies and credentialism.[b] It prepares women for traditional approaches to learning. No discussion of continuing education for women would be complete that did not pay its respects to the other more nontraditional forms it may take in this day and age. Some women, tired of going cap-in-hand to the male decisionmakers who guard the gates of academic credentialism, are continuing their own education by themselves along lines that suit them best.

As an example, I refer to one enterprise that has proved itself successful even in establishment terms, namely the book written by the Boston Women's Health Book Collective, *Our Bodies, Ourselves* [1971]. The authors researched and studied by themselves and wrote this "dissertation." That was women's continuing self-education of a high

---

[b]Still one cannot overlook the readiness at the University of Wisconsin to serve people outside of the University which led to ties with Tribal Women, with labor-union women, with the Women's Political Caucus, and the ERA Coalition, among other groups.

caliber. Another example is a recording company—Olivia Records—which is set up to offer, among other things, "training in the technical, musical, and other fields related to the recording industry and ... jobs with decent pay in non-oppressive conditions."[13] Or, still another, the Washington Area Feminist Theatre which teaches the theater production arts. There are other publishing and theatrical collectives whose members continue both their own education and that of others.

Reuben Hill in an informal discussion once suggested that communes might be serving as educational agencies for some young people. I might mention the educational potential of one of the communes I know best, namely Twin Oaks, in Virginia. It has constituted an unsurpassed form of continuing education for young women and even adult women. Such experience in "accredited communes"might well become acceptable for one's academic "account."

Notes

1. On the basis of a detailed analysis of California data, June Sklar and Beth Berkov (1975) conclude that a rise in the birth rate is now imminent. They believe women have been delaying motherhood, not foregoing it.

2. Among women sixteen to twenty-four not in the labor force, about the same proportion were in school in 1974 as were keeping house, representing a considerable decline in the difference since 1967. At that time, the difference was 3.5 percentage points (25.7 versus 22.2); in 1974 it was 0.7 percentage points (19.6 versus 18.9) [U.S. Department of Commerce, 1974, p. 20].

3. It is the enormous diversity among programs in content, purpose, and clientele which raises such intractable problems of definition, conceptualization, and classification. Matina Horner classifies offerings in continuing education programs on a functional basis as: personal growth and self-development; intellectual development in the liberal arts tradition; professional development in the career sense; job-skill training, including such modest but essential skills as writing resumes; and refresher-retraining services. (Personal communication)

4. The author also sees women's continuing education programs as a counterbalance to the decline in enrollments of college-age students. This decline, it may be noted, had not yet shown up in college enrollment figures for women in 1974. But a report by the Carnegie Foundation for the Advancement of Teaching in 1975 exhibits considerable concern with the problem of declining enrollments. Like the Women's Bureau,

however, the Carnegie Foundation for the Advancement of Teaching sees "the increasing enrollment of part-time, older adult, and nondegree-credit students" as compensating for the decline among undergraduates [1975, p. 147].

5. Among the innovations introduced by women's continuing education programs, as listed by the Women's Bureau, were: strong emphasis on job counseling, individual assessment and counseling, liberal provision for transfer of credits, flexible scheduling of courses at convenient hours, enrollment on a part-time basis, limited course loads, and provision of job leads or referral services [U.S. Department of Labor, 1974, p. 3].

6. An editorial called "The Cost of a College Education" in *The Washington Post,* May 12, 1975, notes that "there seems to be a widespread inclination among young men to go out into the world and test themselves before returning to the classroom . . . . When they return to formal education, it is likely to be as part-time students in the community college, with their emphasis on general education and vocational programs . . . . The average student (in Virginia community colleges) is now 28 years old." There had already been some "give" even in the prestigious universities. In the 1960s so many undergraduate students were dropping out that provision had to be made for their reentry. In some cases young men were even encouraged to drop out in order to clear up personal difficulties. When, teaching at Princeton in the early 1960s, I protested that one of my students needed help with personal problems or he would have to drop out, I was told that psychiatric services were available—which students in those days were loathe to use—and if he did not choose to use them it would be a good idea for him to drop out. Once he had put his own life in order he could return; he would be tougher and stronger and the University would readmit him. I wonder if the prestigious schools would have been as permissive with young women who also wanted to drop out to put their emotional lives—including marriage and motherhood—in order? Colleges had long since learned to accommodate returning war veterans also.

7. In *Women and the Public Interest* (1971, pp. 179–189), I analyzed career patterns in terms of the relative effect of early, late, and quasi-interruptions.

8. There is strong emphasis on the importance of continuity in the careers of women even during time taken out for children. "During periods when their time for outside work is limited, women should take special care to use their time to advance their career" [Bunting, 1973, p. 211]. And, in the same volume, Dorothy Zinberg warns women that "the constant change in scientific knowledge makes it difficult to drop out even

for short periods without losing touch with the mainstream of significant research" [p. 136].

9. Hilda Kahne tells us that "the increasing emphasis on the need for scientific expertise in the 1950s and 1960s did not seem to influence women in either their undergraduate or graduate school educational choices" [1973, p. 164].

10. I go along with Ms. Zinberg in calling for structural changes. I would not discourage one woman from aspiring to her highest level of achievement because we are in a recession and she may have to take a less prestigious job than her older sister got when she continued her education a decade ago. I have elsewhere [1964, p. viii] expressed my rejection of the idea of women as "resources."

11. Other comments by Ms. Horner are disturbing also. She tells us of senior women who can talk a good liberation line but do not truly understand the implications nor recognize the inconsistency in their thinking about future choices. "Some of the young people in our colleges are able to talk about the new ideology, and yet when they are off their guard about using the language of the new ideology, they show that way down deep neither internal nor external realities have come to bear on their thinking or behavior." She described a meeting in which senior, feminist-oriented women talked about how marriage was not to be a part of their plans for the future, but when pressed about their job or career interests, their answer was a confused "we don't know why you're talking about all these job things in this way—we're not really ever going to have to support ourselves. I think that they themselves were startled by what they said, realizing that some of it didn't really fit, was incompatible with everything they had just been saying." Ms. Horner thinks this lack of integration is a real problem and I agree because, like her, "I can't think of anything more frustrating than believing you have an ideology when you don't have the tools, skills, or the internal dynamics to deal with the new things you value so strongly. [Horner, 1974, p. 5.]

12. And not only on the women themselves but on their children as well! ". . . in most cases the grades of children have gone up at least a letter grade . . . (and) a greater sense of responsibility and cooperation is engendered in the children because it is necessary" [Kline, 1973, p. 167].

13. Dust jacket of record "I Know You Know," sung by Meg Christian.

Epilogue

Societal concerns about the underutilization of talented women in an era when the nation needed all the brainpower it could muster, growing awareness of the trend toward early marriage and childbirth (which meant that many young women either did not get to college at all or did not complete their college education), and strong pressure from adult women in the community as well as in academia—female faculty, staff, students, and alumnae—all these were major forces in the emergence of continuing education for women during the early 1960s. The development of actual programs was usually facilitated by dedicated leaders, supportive administrators, receptive communities and enthusiastic clientele. Money from foundations—and particularly the Carnegie Corporation—gave the initial financial push to many of these programs.

The planning of the programs was usually in the hands of small administrative committees who focused first on obtaining funding and on winning the support of institutional officials. Attempts at assessing the needs of clients were generally an informal part of the planning process. Among the initial objectives of continuing education programs for women were: identifying and meeting the needs of community women, including the provision of counseling services and opportunities for intellectual enrichment; facilitating the reentry of women to school or work, sometimes through special short-term training programs; enabling talented women to pursue advanced professional study; allowing alumnae to complete degrees; and helping young women plan for the future. The programs also aspired (1) to change institutional policies so that they would become more hospitable to nontraditional students, and (2) to influence social attitudes so that they would be more accepting of mature women who returned to school or work.

In the first stages, counseling and advising were offered by all women's continuing education programs, and credit or noncredit courses were available at about half of them. These and other services were gradually expanded as the programs grew, serving larger and more broadly based populations and responding to increased demands for more rigorous academic courses, better vocational counseling information, and more effective job preparation.

Most programs depend upon institutional funds for their financial support, though a sizable number are self-supporting from the tuition and fees they collect. Grants, usually in relatively small amounts for special projects of limited duration, are only a minor source of income for the continued operation of the programs.

Because staff, time, and funds are in short supply, research on and evaluation of the programs tend to be informal and unsystematic. The two

125

primary measures of program success are student evaluations and enrollment figures. Long-range comprehensive research has been attempted only rarely. Although the continuing education programs are a function of the college or university, and the program director reports to an institutional administrator, the majority of programs function with considerable autonomy. The interaction of program directors with administrators in the parent institution is informal and ad hoc.

Financial constraints—especially tight budgets and institutional reluctance to commit funds, both of which make it difficult to expand services or even, in some cases, to be assured of survival—are a big problem for CEW programs. Also a problem are institutional regulations designed for traditional students. Despite these difficulties, the programs generally have a highly positive impact on their clients.

To give the highlights of our empirical findings: Women who participate in CEW programs are a diverse group. The stereotype of the middle-class, middle-aged housewife who, bored with her life, decides to dabble in a little culture, simply does not fit. On the contrary, these women are serious, determined, and frequently pragmatic in their goals, planning to get degrees or certificates and to pursue careers. Those strongly career-oriented women in CEW differ in many respects from other participants. Their views about women's role are nontraditional, and they are more self-confident. Although they are more likely to be dissatisfied with the sole role of housewife, their husbands and children generally approve of their educational and occupational activities. Practically all the women in our sample see their continuing education as beneficial both personally and professionally: Many report profound changes in their self-concept. Although relatively few of these women can be labeled activists, most are favorable toward the women's movement (though some report mixed reactions) and feel that it has had a positive influence on many aspects of their lives.

The woman's return to education has also been good for her family. The children's interest in education has increased as a result of their increased respect for mother and the model she provides. The husband is usually emotionally and financially supportive. In most cases, the marriage has improved, though some married women reported marital tensions and problems caused by their new role and activities. Some husbands mentioned the economic benefits that would accrue from the wife's employment on the basis of her new skills.

Whereas the women's movement has given women the freedom to be, continuing education has given mature women a foundation on which they can build, developing their talents, acquiring skills and knowledge that enable them to enter or reenter the labor market. Other campus efforts—such as women's studies, women's centers, and programmatic research—have also contributed to the greater freedom and increased strength of women.

The very existence of CEW programs gives a psychological boost to the woman who is considering a return to school, assuring her that she is not alone and that she will be meeting and attending classes with women in similar positions who share similar concerns. The programs indicate that, though older than the typical undergraduate, she can still go to college; others like her have done so successfully.

CEW programs are oriented toward the job market and organized to develop the student's capacity for competent job performance. To meet the diverse needs and interests of their clients, most offer both vocational skills training and liberal arts curricula. Counseling and career guidance play key roles in the educational process, but job placement services tend to be inadequate.

The constraints of time and place that generally hamper mature women with outside responsibilities who want to return to college have been greatly reduced by CEW, which has restructured the delivery of courses from, for example, fifty minutes three times a week to a three-hour sequence once a week and has used available space in churches and schools around the community to reduce transportation hassles. Admissions procedures and performance criteria have also been altered so that they are more appropriate to adults.

While many colleges and universities have recognized the demand for continuing education and have developed such programs, support is often qualified. As was indicated, the programs must frequently generate their own funds through tuition and fees rather than relying on the institution. While this arrangement is good in that it ensures that the survival of a program depends on its meeting the needs of its audience, it is unfortunate in that it necessitates charging a high price for courses, with little left over for financial aid or program development. Moreover, most programs are not completely autonomous but depend on the continued favor of an administrator in the parent institution. Financial success and administrative approval are essential to a program's continuation.

Continuing education programs for women clearly point to the need for institutional change. Colleges and universities must adopt a more flexible attitude to accommodate individual differences. They must relax nonessential academic regulations and requirements that have no real meaning when applied to older women returning to college. CEW is in the forefront of higher education innovation, demonstrating that changes can be made with no sacrifice of quality. By working to remove structural and institutional barriers as well as to alleviate some of the problems and concerns of the populations they serve, they have earned our support and approval.

Appendixes

Appendix A
Sample and Procedures

Fifteen continuing education programs were selected to represent the diversity of existing programs. The parent institutions include two-year colleges, four-year colleges, and universities; coeducational and primarily single-sex institutions; public and private sectarian and nonsectarian control; rural and urban settings; and homogeneous and mixed populations. Some of the programs were large and multifaceted, others small and single-focused. Three of the earliest pioneer programs were included in the sample, as was one program based not in a higher educational institution but in a state system of higher education. Two of the fourteen institutionally based programs were located at the same institution. Thus, the sample comprises thirteen parent institutions and one state system.

Table A–1 lists the characteristics of these sample institutions. Three were private universities, including one affiliated with the state; three were private colleges (one Catholic women's college, one nonsectarian women's college, and one coeducational college); one was in a private cluster-college system; five were state universities, and one was a two-year residential college. With respect to regional location, one was Southern, six Midwestern, three Western, and five Eastern. The sample includes very old institutions (founded in 1819) and relatively new ones (founded in 1963). Their fall 1970 enrollments ranged from 391 to 38,106. Revenues ranged from about 3 million dollars to 258 million dollars (figures for the 1970–1971 academic year). The types of students these institutions serve varied greatly. The two-year residential college had a relatively large nonwhite enrollment (23 percent Spanish heritage, 12 percent black). Two of the institutions, located in the same state and part of the same system, differed in that though both offer undergraduate programs, one campus has numerous graduate programs and also offers professional degrees while the other is limited to graduate courses.

Once the institutions and programs had been identified, a letter of invitation was sent, early in April 1974, to the director of each program, with a copy going to the president or chancellor of the parent institution. All the programs accepted our invitation.

131

Table A-1
Characteristics of Parent Institutions and CEW Programs

Type of Institution	Location of Institution	Enrollment of Institution [a]	Year CEW Program Began	Enrollment of CEW Program [b]	CEW Program Offerings [c]
State residential junior college	Southeast	38,106	1965	Large	Counseling, noncredit classes, workshops
Private coeducational university	East	14,998	1964	Medium	Group and individual counseling, noncredit and credit courses, degree and certificate programs, workshops, and scholarships
Private Catholic women's liberal arts college	Midwest	1,311	1965	Small	Counseling, degree program, noncredit and credit courses, certificate program in management
Coeducational state university	Midwest	9,681	1966	Large	Individual and group counseling, noncredit courses, workshops
Coeducational state university	Midwest	9,515	1963	Medium	Counseling, noncredit courses, workshops
Private coeducational university	Northeast	18,536	1963	Small	Counseling, noncredit courses, Extension degree
Private coeducational liberal arts college	Northeast	840	1962	Small	Counseling, Bachelor's degree, professional programs in college teaching and medical genetics
Coeducational state university and land-grant college	Midwest	51,442	1960	Large	Credit and noncredit courses
			1960[d]	Small	Counseling, noncredit courses

					Counseling
Private, coeducational state-related university	Northeast	31,259	1964	Medium	Group and individual counseling, credit courses, degree program
Coeducational state university	Midwest	34,702	1964	Large	Counseling, credit and noncredit seminars, fellowships
Private, liberal arts college for women	Northeast	1,243	1960	Medium	Group and individual counseling, credit and noncredit courses, certificate programs
Coeducational state university	West	29,093	1966	Large	Counseling, colloquia (credit), graduate programs: liberal studies and internships for women in administration
Private cluster colleges (6)	West	541-1,325	1966	Small	Group counseling, credit and noncredit courses, workshops, in-service training
	Weste		1966	Medium	

Source: Furniss, W. Todd, ed., *American Universities and Colleges*, ACE, 11th ed., Washington, D.C., 1973. Information was obtained from Cass, J., and Birnbaum, M., *Comparative Guide to Junior and Two-Year Community Colleges*, New York: Harper and Row, 1972, for the first school.

[a]Enrollments are given for Fall, 1970, undergraduate and graduate.

[b]It was very difficult to get exact enrollment sizes. Thus the CEW programs were divided into the following categories: Small (250 and under), Medium (251-999), and Large (1,000 and above).

[c]This list is not comprehensive. Only the major program components are included.

[d]These two programs are located at the same institution.

[e]This program was not based in a higher educational institution but in the state system of higher education.

First Phase

The first phase of the project called for case studies of each of the fifteen selected programs. A sheet was sent to each program director requesting information about the program's history, personnel, structure, facilities, program, and enrollees. These completed forms provided background material so that the research team would have some familiarity with the general conformation of each program prior to their visits. The case studies, then, were conducted through site visits to the programs during which in-depth interviews were conducted with a variety of people: two administrators in the parent institution, one being the administrator directly responsible for the program, the other usually the chief executive (president or chancellor); the program director; a faculty member teaching in the program; and a counselor working with women. In addition, each program randomly selected the names of women who had participated or were participating in various program components: e.g., group counseling, credit and noncredit courses, and certificate degree programs. Interviews with five alumnae of each program, fifteen women currently participating in it, five spouses of participating women, and at least five of their children concluded the case studies.

The interview form used with participants and alumnae of the program inquired into their personal background, their educational and occupational history prior to contact with the program, and their experiences as an enrollee in CEW, including: (1) the factors that prompted their enrollment, their reasons for choosing the particular program, and their objectives in returning to school; (2) their assessment of the program; (3) the factors that facilitated and those that impeded their progress; and (4) the influence and effects of their experience in CEW on themselves and on their families. Women enrolled in degree or certificate programs were asked a series of questions about that component. The form for alumnae had an additional section designed to get at their experiences after leaving the program.

Husbands were asked how they perceived their wife's involvement in CEW: why she had enrolled and what her goals were; what they felt about her decision; how it had affected family life (including what possible benefits they anticipated from the wife's educational attainment or employment); and how they felt about the women's movement. Background information was also obtained from husbands. Similarly, children were asked about their own educational achievements and aspirations; their perceptions of mother's reasons for, and objectives in, returning to school; their feelings about her involvement in the program; their perceptions and feelings about changes at home as a result of this involvement; and their understanding of, and response to, the women's movement.

The interview form used with the director of the continuing education program investigated the program's history and development, its structure, the personnel involved, admissions requirements and financial aid available to returning women, the kinds of enrollees recruited, and the quality of their performance. In addition, they were asked to assess both the quality of the program itself and its impact on the larger institution and community. Finally, they were asked to indicate their personal background, their objectives for the program, and their contributions to it.

In the case of faculty members and counselors, questions covered five areas: their position in the program; its structure and administration; the program component with which they were affiliated (counseling or course work); the academic preparation of and the problems faced by the enrollees; and their assessment of the program.

Administrators were asked about the program's inception (including what role they had played in it); about the program's structure; their contact with the women in the program and their perception of enrollees' progress and problems or needs; their assessment of the program and its impact on the larger institution; and their views as to the future of the program.

Although Helen S. Astin, the project's director, and two of her associates, Carole Leland and Joseph Katz, were responsible for the conduct of the interviewing process, additional interviewers were hired to assist at a number of programs. The mean age of these interviewers was forty-two, with a range from twenty-five to fifty-seven. All but one had a bachelor's degree, about half had a master's (usually in counseling and guidance), and all had training or experience in interviewing. Most had worked in education as teachers, counselors, or administrators; some had research experience. Instructions to the interviewers were formulated to assure uniformity in conducting the interviews; they were asked to make it clear to the interviewees that the study was a national one and that the interviewer did not represent the CEW program itself. When asked for their comments after the interview experience, most of the interviewers mentioned the interest and cooperative attitudes of the women, several said they found some redundancy in the questions, and almost half brought up the difficulty of interviewing women who had only slight contact with the program.

Finally, where interviewers were employed, the program director provided further information about how both interviewers and interviewees were selected. Thus, it was verified that the participants and alumnae had been randomly selected and that the continuing education program office had invited these women to participate, either by letter, with a follow-up phone call, or directly through a telephone call. The interviewers were selected either by one of the project associates or by a staff member of the CEW program.

All the case studies were supervised directly either by the project director or by one of the project associates, thus involving each member of the research team in collecting data through interviews. This phase took place during the spring and summer of 1974. In all, 212 participants, 67 alumnae, 77 spouses, and 88 children were interviewed. After their responses had been tabulated, coding categories were developed for the open-ended interview forms used with each of these four groups of respondents. In addition, twenty-seven interviews were completed with institutional administrators and forty-two with program staff (seventeen directors (in two of the programs both the past and current director were interviewed); fourteen counselors, and twelve faculty members).

Second Phase

The second phase of the study, carried out in the fall and early winter of 1974, was a mail survey of respondents, participants, and spouses. Based on the experience gained during the interviews and during the later development of coding categories, a 65-item precoded questionnaire was devised to survey participants and alumnae. Because the questionnaire was designed to be answered by both participants and alumnae, and both by women working on degrees and certificates and by women who were not, optional sections (to be completed or not, according to the respondent's status) were included in the questionnaire. A second precoded questionnaire was devised for the husbands of participants. To explain the study and its purpose and to request their assistance, cover letters to accompany the survey form were composed for each of the three groups.

Early in September, a letter was mailed to each program's director requesting assistance in the sample selection and outlining the criteria that had been established as a framework for this selection. For purposes of this phase of the study, *alumnae* were defined as women who had participated in a program in the previous two to five years but were not currently receiving any services from the program. Thus, a random sample was solicited from each program, varying from 50 to 110 names. The sample size and the number of years investigated depended on the length of time the program had been in operation, its size, and the components it offered. *Participants* were defined as all women (including those with prior program contact) who entered or reentered the program (by enrollment or for one-time counseling or information) during July, August, and September of 1974. Each program was requested to send a list of *all* such participants, unless the number of current enrollees exceeded 150, in which case the programs were asked to select a random sample of 150 names. The name, address, and year (in the case of alumnae) or month (in the case of participants) of first contact with the program, the program component affiliation, and the spouse's name (if available) were obtained for both participants and alumnae.

During November of 1974, the questionnaires, entitled "National Survey of Women in Continuing Education Programs," were mailed in staggered format (we had not yet received lists from all the participating programs and also we wanted to bypass the holiday week) to approximately equal numbers of participants and alumnae. In cases where the program had sent a list of more than sixty-seven names (the per-program allotment for each of the two groups), sixty-seven were randomly selected for the mailing; if the program had not submitted enough names, then the lists of the larger programs were used to supply this deficiency. The total numbers of questionnaires mailed were 999 to participants, and 992 to alumnae.

The names of spouses were more difficult to obtain, being unavailable from the records of some programs and only unsystematically available from the records of others. All the names of participants' spouses provided on the lists were used for the sample, which totaled 290. The questionnaires to husbands were mailed during the first week of December.

A sizable number of alumnae questionnaires (130) were returned as undeliverable; so alternate alumnae were sampled and seventy-nine new questionnaires were mailed. From three to six weeks after the first mailing, a second questionnaire was sent to all nonrespondents. The two mailouts yielded the following rates of return:

1.   Participants: 68 percent ($N = 660$). Twenty questionnaires were returned as undeliverable, fifteen were returned because the questionnaire was regarded as nonapplicable or because the addressee was deceased.
2.   Alumnae: 61 percent ($N = 540$). There were 83 undeliverables, and 21 questionnaires were returned as nonapplicable.
3.   Spouses: 54 percent ($N = 153$). Five were undeliverable, and four were returned as nonapplicable.

At the close of the survey, we decided to follow up a small subsample to determine possible reasons for nonresponse and to identify the background characteristics of nonrespondents. Fifteen nonrespondents who happened to be in the Los Angeles area (where the project was carried out) were reached by telephone; and fifty-two (two alumnae and two participants from each of the remaining thirteen programs) were sent a letter. Of the fifteen reached by telephone, eight mailed in the original full-length questionnaire, three agreed to return it but failed to do so, three said they preferred not to participate, and one said she would respond to the few brief questions in the letter sent to the sample of fifty-two. From the telephone interviews, we learned that nonrespondents were similar in background characteristics to respondents. The reasons for nonresponse included lack of interest, lack of time, the feeling that the questionnaire was too personal, and confusion among women who had participated in several kinds of adult learning experience as to which program the questionnaire applied.

Of those who received the letter, seventeen (nine participants and eight alumnae) responded. The reasons they cited for returning to school were the same as those given by respondents to the full-length questionnaire: to obtain an education, to earn a degree, to pursue interests, and to enrich themselves. Ten of the seventeen reported they were no longer affiliated with any program, but two were planning to return to school in the near future. Of those in a program, two were working toward the baccalaureate. Of the total group of seventeen letter respondents, eight were employed, and an additional five planned to return to work. Ten were currently married. Their ages ranged from twenty to seventy years. In sum, the profile of the seventeen nonrespondents corresponds closely to the profile that emerged from the questionnaire data.

The method of analysis included frequency distributions, cross tabulations, and regression analysis.

Appendix B
Historical Notes on the American Council on Education's Involvement with the Concerns of Women in Higher Education

1. *Committee on Training of Women for Public Service*

    In 1920, the American Council on Education established a standing committee on the Training of Women for Public Service. (The name was changed later in the same year to Committee on Training of Women for Professional Service.) Gertrude S. Martin of Cornell University was named Chairperson of the Committee.

    In the April 1920 issue of the *Educational Record* Elizabeth Kemper Adams wrote an article entitled "Some New Professional Standards for College Women," which discussed training for professional service in a type of apprenticeship, a program which resembles the internship programs of today.

    For the 1921 Annual Meeting Elizabeth Kemper Adams prepared a report describing several independent agencies engaged in studying occupations for women and methods of placement.

    The Annual Report of 1922 stated that there was a committee preparing to study careers of women holders of the doctor's degree for the Pan American International Committee of Women.

    During the 1930s, the Council took no actions and made no reports on the status of women.

    In January 1940, Marion E. Park, President of Bryn Mawr College, wrote an article for the *Educational Record* entitled "Some Values of Progressive Education for Women." The article was a discussion of sex stereotyping and its deleterious effects on the education of women.

2. *Women in the Defense Decade*

    During World War II and the Korean War, interest in women was concentrated on the question of women's service in the defense of the country. In 1951, the Council sponsored a national conference on Women in the Defense Decade. Nine hundred women and men came together to consider "the responsibilities and opportunities" for women in the coming decade. The Honorable Mary H. Donlon, Judge, United States Customs Court, chaired the conference which resulted in a publication entitled "Women in the Defense Decade" and the establishment of a continuing committee within ACE.

Prepared by the ACE Office of Women in Higher Education

3. *1953 Commission on the Education of Women*

In 1952, Kathryn S. Phillips, first president of the National Association of Women Deans and Counselors (now called the National Association of Women Deans, Administrators, and Counselors), voiced her concern at the Association's Annual Meeting as to "whether women faculty and students were working at the height, depth and breadth of their capacities." The American Council on Education, in February of 1953, with the assistance of the Ellis Phillips Foundation, brought together the concerns of Ms. Phillips and the continuing committee in the formation of a Commission on the Education of Women.

During the eight-year duration of the Commission, its Directors and Chairpersons were as follows:

	Director	Chairperson
1953	Althea Hottel	Esther Lloyd-Jones
1954	Althea Hottel	Esther Lloyd-Jones
1955	Althea Hottel	Esther Lloyd-Jones
1956		Esther Lloyd-Jones
1957		Esther Lloyd-Jones
1958	Opal David	Mary H. Donlon
1959	Opal David	Mary I. Bunting, President of Radcliffe
1960	Opal David	Margaret Culkin Banning, Author
1961	Opal David	Margaret Habein, Dean of Fairmount College Municipal University of Wichita

Esther Lloyd-Jones, the first Chairperson of the Commission, was Professor of Education at Teachers College, Columbia University. Althea Hottel, the first Director of the Commission, was Dean of Women at the University of Pennsylvania and a former AAUW President. During her two years in office, Dr. Hottel prepared an interim report on the Commission's work, entitled *How Fare American Women?, 1955*.

In 1953, the Commission consulted with seven social scientists from anthropology, child development, psychology, social psychology and sociology. Drawing on this, as well as their own three-day conference, the Commission outlined seven major purposes:

. . . to study the roles of women in American society and the sources of confusion in these roles; to observe the influences that education, social attitudes, and cultural patterns have had upon women in the development of their personalities, the use of their aptitudes and the nature of their contributions; to ascertain the differentials in child rearing and their effects on the personality, the aptitudes, attitudes, and responses of both sexes; to examine the motivation and basic processes that affect the intellectual growth of men and women; to determine what social factors inhibit, permit, or encourage the larger participation of women in the familial, economic, civic, and cultural life of this country; to determine what changes in roles men and women view as desirable and how these are related to definable trends; and from all of the above to make recommendations for change for the thoughtful consideration and action of the American people.

In 1954, the Commission sponsored research designed by Robin Williams and John Dean of Cornell on "Social and Cultural Factors Affecting Role-Conflict and Adjustment Among American Women" and another study by Marie Jahoda, Professor of Psychology and Associate Director of Research Center for Human Relations in New York City, on "Psychological Problems of Women in Different Social Roles: An Exploratory Case Study." Both of these studies were funded by the National Institutes of Health. In addition, three very important doctoral studies were stimulated by the Commission. They are: (1) "A Study of the Concerns of a Selected Group of Unmarried Women," by Helen Whiteside, Director of the College Union and Union Residencies at New York State University at New Paltz; (2) "An Exploration of the Needs of Freshmen and Sophomore Women College Students for Life Planning," by Jane Berry, Director of Undergraduate Placement at Hunter College; (3) "A Study of What Negro Women College Graduates Think of Their College Education" by Jeanne Noble, Assistant Professor at New York University.

4. *1957 Conference on the Present Status and Prospective Trends of Research on the Education of Women*

In 1957, the Commission, directed by Opal D. David, staff of Washington office of Public Administration Clearinghouse, and chaired by Katherine McBride, President of Bryn Mawr College, held a conference on research on the education of women. This conference resulted in the publication, *The Education of Women: Signs for the Future.* Jean Campbell, Director of the University of Michigan Center for the Continuing Education of Women, in her paper in Alice Rossi and Ann Calderwood's book, *Academic Women on the Move* (1973) refers to this meeting as a "landmark conference." She further states that "statistics concerning the number of women enrolled in higher education, their employment, and life span, and the discontinuities in their lives were made clearly apparent."

5. *Intercollegiate Association of Women Students*

Sue Storer, President of Associate Women Students at Purdue University, prepared a report on women students and sent it to the IAWS membership. Esther Lloyd-Jones included this in the Commission's Annual Report.

6. *Bulletin — "The Education of Women"*

A bulletin on "The Education of Women" was published by ACE from 1958–1961.

7. *The Span of a Woman's Life and Learning*

A general policy statement called "The Span of a Woman's Life and Learning" was published in April 1960. This statement identified a number of areas where greater emphasis was needed to encourage women in development of their full potential.

In 1960, an invitational conference on "Counseling Girls: High School and College" was held. A second conference on counseling was held in 1961, and a report was published in *The School Counselor,* October 1961.

8. *Itasca Conference*

The Carnegie Corporation made a $23,000 grant to the Council for a conference on the continuing education of women. The conference was held in 1962 with three papers published in the Educational Record of October 1961 serving as discussion papers. The final proceedings of this conference were published in an ACE book, *Education and a Woman's Life.*

9. *Discontinuation*

December 1961 marked the discontinuation of the Commission on the Education of Women.

10. *Sex Discrimination*

1970 and 1972 brought forth two ACE special reports on the Executive Order 11246 (amended by 11375); Title VII of the Civil Rights Act of 1964 as amended by the Equal Employment Opportunity Act; the Equal Pay Act of 1963; Title IX of the Education Amendments of 1972; and finally, Titles VII and VIII of the Public Health Service Act as amended by the Comprehensive Health Manpower Act and the Nurse Training Amendments Act of 1971. These two reports were distributed to the ACE membership.

11. *Women in Higher Education*

The 55th Annual Meeting of the Council was developed around the theme "Women in Higher Education." Background papers for the conference have been published in a volume entitled *Women in Higher Education.*

12. *Chairpersons of the American Council on Education*

Four women have been elected to serve as chairpersons of the Council: Virginia Gildersleeve, President of Barnard College, 1926–27; Katherine E. McBride, President of Bryn Mawr College, 1955–56; Martha Peterson, President of Barnard College, 1972–73; and Sister Ann Ida Gannon, President of Mundelein College, 1973–74.

13. *Office of Women in Higher Education*

In January 1972, Roger Heyns, the new president of ACE, and Martha Peterson, chairperson, instituted discussions with professional women educators. From these discussions emerged a decision, approved by the ACE Board of Directors in October 1972, to establish an Office of Women in Higher Education within the Council.

Dr. Nancy Schlossberg, Associate Professor of Education at Wayne State University, became the director of the Office in May, 1973. Members of the Commission on Women in Higher Education were appointed in October 1973 with Patricia Roberts Harris, Attorney with Fried, Frank, Harris, Shriver & Kampleman, as Chairperson.

After consultation with the Commission, ACE staff, individual women and women's groups concerned with higher education, and various programs offered by the Office, four areas of concern for improving the status of women in higher education were identified. These concerns included:

- Affirmative action and technical assistance to women, to institutions, and to government
- Coordination of groups focusing on women in higher education
- Coordination and involvement in ACE programs and activities concerned with women

with the major focus on women in higher education administration, specifically on a study and action program designed to increase the numbers and enhance the skills of women in administrative positions in colleges and universities.

Dr. Emily Taylor, former Dean of Women and Director of the Women's Resource Center at the University of Kansas, became the director of the Office in January 1975.

During the two years of its existence, the Office has been instrumental in the formation of a coalition of women's and educational groups concerned with women's education, has served on the Council's Equal Employment Opportunity Task Force, has delivered testimony and worked for the implementation of the Women's Educational Equity Act (Title IV of the Elementary and Secondary Education Act extension bill) and Title IX of the Education Amendments of 1972; staff members have appeared as speakers and workshop leaders on behalf of women and initiated a series of analyses of the status of women in higher education administration. In addition the following programs were given by the Office:

- Workshop for Women Considering Careers in College and University Administration (with the Office of Leadership Development in Higher Education)
- Workshop on Freeing Sex Roles for New Careers
- Invitational Seminar on Identification, Recommendation, and Placement of Women in Higher Education Administration

Source Material

1920–1951
Educational Record (included reports from the Annual Meetings of the ACE)

1952
Raymond F. Howes, ed., *Women in the Defense Decade,* Report of a national conference of persons representing schools, colleges, and universities, government agencies, and selected national organizations, New York City, September 27–28, 1951, series I, no. 52, reports of committees and conferences, Washington, DC: ACE, April 1952.

1955
Althea K. Hottel, *How Fare American Women?,* A report of the Commission on the Education of Women, Washington, DC: ACE, 1955.

1959
Opal D. David, ed., *The Education of Women: Signs for the Future,* Report of a conference on the present status and prospective trends of research on the education of women, sponsored by the American Council on Education, Rye, New York, October 27–30, 1957, Washington, DC: ACE, 1959.

1963
Lawrence E. Dennis, ed., *Education and a Women's Life,* Proceedings of the Itasca Conference on the Continuing Education of Women, Itasca State Park, Minnesota, April 1960, Washington, DC: ACE, 1963.

1968
Charles G. Dobbins, ed., *American Council on Education Leadership and Chronology 1918-1968,* Washington, DC: ACE, 1968.

1970
"Discrimination Against Women in Colleges," ACE Special Report by the Commission on Federal Relations, September 1970.

1972

ACE Special Report, April 1972

Roger W. Heyns, "Sex Discrimination and Contract Compliance: Beyond the Legal Requirements"

Betty Pryor, "Legal Regulations on Sex Discrimination"

Bernice Sandler and Sheldon Steinbach, "HEW Contract Compliance — Major Concerns of Institutions."

Women in Higher Education, Background papers for participants in the 55th Annual Meeting of the American Council on Education, October 1972, Washington, DC: ACE, 1972 (essays will be combined with others to be published in a book, 1973).

W. Todd Furniss, ed., *Women in Higher Education,* to be published in 1973.

Alice S. Rossi and Ann Calderwood, eds., *Academic Women on the Move,* New York: Russell Sage Foundation, 1973.

1974

Nancy K. Schlossberg, Donna Shavlik and Nancy McBride. "Equal Benefits in Retirement — A Case for Equity." Duplicated. Washington: American Council on Education, Office of Women in Higher Education, January 14, 1974.

Nancy A. McBride, *Report: Workshop for Women Considering Careers in College and University Administration.* Washington: American Council on Education, Office of Women in Higher Education, and Institute for College and University Administrators, 1974.

Appendix C

Frequency Distributions

Percentage Distribution of Responses to the Questionnaire Items

I. *Background Information*

1. | Age | Participants | Alumnae |
   |---|---|---|
   | 20 or under | 2 | 0 |
   | 21-25 | 12 | 8 |
   | 26-30 | 18 | 12 |
   | 31-35 | 17 | 13 |
   | 36-40 | 16 | 18 |
   | 41-45 | 10 | 18 |
   | 46-50 | 12 | 13 |
   | 51-55 | 8 | 9 |
   | 56-60 | 4 | 6 |
   | 61-65 | 1 | 3 |
   | 66 or over | 2 | 1 |

2. | Ethnic/racial background | Participants | Alumnae |
   |---|---|---|
   | White | 94 | 95 |
   | Black | 3 | 3 |
   | Asian American | 1 | 0 |
   | American Indian | 1 | 0 |
   | Spanish-speaking (Mexican American, Puerto Rican, Cuban) | 1 | 1 |

3. | Religious Background and Preference | Religion Raised in | | Current Religion | |
   |---|---|---|---|---|
   | | P | A | P | A |
   | Protestant | 52 | 52 | 35 | 36 |
   | Catholic | 25 | 23 | 17 | 15 |
   | Jewish | 16 | 18 | 14 | 14 |
   | Other | 3 | 3 | 6 | 7 |
   | None | 3 | 3 | 23 | 20 |
   | No answer | 1 | 1 | 7 | 8 |

4. What formal education did your parents have?

	Mother		Father	
	P	A	P	A
Less than high school	19	22	21	22
Some high school	11	12	11	11
High school diploma	30	25	19	16
Trade, business, or technical school	8	8	8	7
Some college	17	16	13	14
College graduate	9	12	11	11
Some graduate work	3	2	3	2
Graduate or professional degree	4	4	14	16

5. Did your mother work while you were growing up (before you were 18)?

	P	A
Yes	44	42
No	56	58

147

6. What were your parents' jobs? (circle the category that most nearly applies to the kind of work done for the longest period of time/most recently)

	Mother		Father	
	P	A	P	A
Arts (performing and creative, including crafts)	3	3	1	1
Business (administrator, manager)	2	2	10	12
Business (owner, consultant, accountant)	3	5	20	21
Business (sales, public relations, advertising)	5	4	11	10
Clerical and related fields (secretary, bookkeeper, cashier)	19	17	1	1
Clergy, religious work	0	0	1	1
Dressmaking, alterations and tailoring	3	4	1	1
Engineering and architecture	0	0	5	4
Farming, ranching	1	2	5	7
Health fields—non-MD (nurse, therapist, assistant)	4	3	1	0
Military	0	0	2	2
Professions (law, medicine, psychology)	0	1	8	8
Public administrator or official	0	0	2	2
Research scientist (chemist, economist)	0	0	1	1
Semiskilled or unskilled work (factory work, waitress, truck driver)	11	9	10	10
Skilled or technical trades (beautician, carpenter, mechanic)	1	2	17	13
Social work, counseling	1	3	0	1
Teaching: private lessons (music, language)	1	1	0	0
Teaching or educational administration (other than college level)	7	6	1	2
Teaching or educational administration (college level)	1	1	1	2
Other _____ (specify)	0	1	1	1
None	36	35	0	1

7. Are you currently:

	P	A
Single (never married)	17	11
Married (once only)	58	63
Married (remarried)	8	9
Separated	3	2
Divorced	12	12
Widowed	3	3

If ever married:

8. How many children do you have?

	P	A
1	17	14
2	36	32
3	29	29
4	12	16
5	3	6
6 or more	3	3

9. Indicate whether you have children in any of the following age categories:

	P	A
Birth-5	24	14
6-12	40	36
13-17	35	39
18-22	28	31
23+	21	26

10. Husband's education (highest level attained):

	P	A
Less than high school diploma	4	3
High school diploma	7	8
Some college	16	10
Associate of Arts degree	1	1
Bachelor's	27	29
Master's	16	17
Doctorate (PhD, EdD)	7	12
Professional degree (MD, DDS, LLB, JD)	18	17
Other (including technical or trade school)	4	4

11. What is your husband's occupation?

	P	A
Retired	2	5
Student	3	3
Arts (performing and creative)	2	2
Business (administrator, manager)	16	18
Business (owner, consultant, accountant)	11	12
Business (sales, public relations, advertising)	9	7
Computer-related fields (programmer, systems analyst)	2	2
Counseling, social work	2	1
Engineering, architecture	11	8
Law	10	6
Medicine, dentistry	5	8
Other professions (pharmacist, optometrist, clinical psychologist)	3	4
Scientific research (chemist, economist)	3	3
Semiskilled or unskilled work	3	2

Skilled or technical trades	8	4
Teaching or educational administration (other than college level)	3	3
Teaching or educational administration (college level)	6	8
Other _____	3	5

12. What is the approximate family income?

	Husband's		Yours	
	P	*A*	*P*	*A*
None	2	2	40	36
$4,999 or less	3	3	17	17
$5,000-9,999	7	4	24	22
$10,000-14,999	20	15	14	18
$15,000-19,999	17	16	3	5
$20,000-29,999	24	24	2	2
$30,000-39,999	12	15	0	0
$40,000 or more	16	22	0	1

II. *This section deals with questions regarding your education and work experience before you had any contact with the continuing education program*

13. Highest level of education:

	P	*A*
Less than high school diploma	1	1
High school diploma	13	8
Technical or business school	7	8
Some college	30	33
Associate of Arts degree	4	4
Bachelor's	34	37
Master's	9	8
Doctorate (Phd, EdD)	1	1
Professional (MD, DDS, LLB, JD)	0	0
Other _____	1	0

14. If you attended or completed college, what was your field of study?

	P	*A*
Arts and humanities	27	29
Business (merchandising, business administration)	8	5
Education	16	16
General studies or liberal arts	20	19
Health fields—non-MD (nursing, home economics, recreation)	11	8
Medicine, dentistry, law	1	1
Natural sciences and mathematics	2	3
Social sciences (social work, sociology, psychology, economics)	14	18
Other _____	1	1

15. What was your approximate grade average?

	High School		College	
	P	A	P	A
A	32	33	13	13
B	52	53	50	54
C	15	13	18	17
Below C	0	0	1	2
Does not apply	1	0	18	16

16. If you did not attend or complete college, indicate the primary reason:

Attended a noncollegiate institution	9	8
Wanted to work	13	12
Funds not available	34	32
Illness (personal, family)	2	1
Lack of interest or motivation	16	14
Marriage, pregnancy	25	34

17. Indicate the types of volunteer work you have been involved in:

	P	A
None	11	8
Arts (museum, symphony	17	23
Charities, fund raising (not elsewhere classified)	47	51
Churches	48	56
Community organizations	53	58
Handicapped	18	19
Hospitals, clinics, nursing homes	28	30
Politics	33	37
Professional organizations	20	19
Schools, colleges, including alumnae activities	40	43
Social issues groups (civil rights, ecology, consumer affairs, women's movement)	31	38

III. *Employment (Paid)*

18. Please circle one under each column:

	Job prior to any contact with the program		Current Job		Job you would ultimately like to have	
	P	A	P	A	P	A
None	8	12	47	46	8	7
Arts (creative and performing, including crafts)	3	3	1	2	7	5
Business (administrator, manager)	4	4	2	3	7	7
Business (owner, consultant, accountant)	1	2	2	2	3	3
Business (sales, public relations, advertising)	7	5	3	4	4	2

Clerical and related fields (secretary, bookkeeper, cashier)	31	31	16	11	3	1
Community work, politics	1	2	1	0	3	4
Counseling, social work, therapist, clinical psychologist	3	4	3	3	20	20
Editing, publications, writing	3	3	2	3	8	8
Health Fields—non-MD (nursing, therapist, assistant)	8	8	6	4	7	6
Library work	2	2	1	2	2	4
Professions (law, medicine, engineering, architecture, pharmacy)	1	1	1	2	8	9
Recreation work	0	1	0	1	1	1
Scientific research (chemist, economist)	1	2	1	1	2	2
Semiskilled or unskilled work (factory work, waitress)	3	2	2	1	0	0
Skilled and technical trades (beautician, draftsman, seamstress)	2	2	2	1	1	0
Teaching: private lessons (music, languages)	1	1	1	0	1	1
Teaching or educational administration or staff (other than college level)	15	12	5	7	6	9
Teaching or educational administration or staff (college level)	4	3	3	4	8	8
Other _____	1	1	2	3	3	4

19. Please circle the appropriate choice in each column for the above jobs:

	Prior		Current		Future	
	P	*A*	*P*	*A*	*P*	*A*
Full-time	72	67	37	34	63	59
Part-time	19	19	17	19	26	30
Does not apply	10	14	46	47	12	11

20. If you are not currently working, please circle your *one primary* reason:

	P	A
Looking for work	7	5
I am in school/training for work	27	32
No desire to work	9	7
No financial need to work	19	17
Scarce job opportunities in my field	3	4
Inadequate training or experience for a job	7	10
Husband's objections or preferences	2	3
Difficulties and costs of household maintenance or child care	2	3
Children's needs and preferences; pregnancy	18	15
Other _____	7	4

IV. *This section deals primarily with questions concerning your experience while in contact with the continuing education program.*

21. When you made your *first* contact with the program, how long had it been since you last took any credit or noncredit course?

	P	A
Less than 1 year	28	24
1-5	35	32
6-10	15	13
11-15	6	11
16-20	7	11
21-30	6	7
More than 30 years	3	3

22. When you came to the Continuing Education program, how important was each of the following *objectives?*

	Very Important	
	P	A
To prepare for a better job	44	42
To become more educated	63	62
To receive a degree, certificate, or college credit	29	35
To assess myself academically	26	31
To receive counseling, testing, information	35	31
To make contact with other people	24	20
To achieve independence and a sense of identity	44	43
To develop skills to become more effective in my family or community	34	33
To be involved in women's programs or issues	10	8
To obtain financial assistance	10	8

23. Please indicate the importance of each of the following *reasons* or *factors* in your coming to the program:

Very important

	P	A
Dissatisfied with my job	22	20
Bored at home	18	21
Lessening of home responsibilities	16	20
Family or marital problems (including divorce)	10	9
Serious illness or death in family	4	4
The program's offerings	61	56
My move to this location/community	7	7
The availability of funds	13	10
Encouragement and/or recommendation from others	33	29

24. How did you first learn about the program?

	P	A
Word of mouth	44	41
Media (TV, radio, newspaper)	17	19
Program advertising (pamphlets, meetings, direct contact)	26	20
Contact with the parent institution	13	21

25. What have your contacts with the Program consisted of?

	Past		Current
	P	A	P
Information	68	79	23
Referral	25	27	2
Testing	24	29	2
Financial aid	6	10	4
Group counseling	11	16	5
Individual counseling (more than once)	13	22	5
Certificate program	8	16	7
Degree program	16	17	11
Noncredit courses	27	39	21
Credit courses/seminars	28	39	14
Workshop(s)	15	21	5
In-service training (within the Program or at outside agency)	6	8	3

26. Indicate the ways in which your contact and experience with the program have influenced you.

	P	A
Provided focus and direction	32	30
I feel more confused about my goals	3	3
Gave me confidence, increased self-esteem	32	38

	P	A
Decreased my self-confidence	2	1
Informed me of alternatives and options	30	29
Provided a catalyst or means to pursue further education	31	35
Caused me to seek employment	5	13
Made me decide my place is at home	1	1
I feel better educated	29	36
I have developed employable skills	13	20
Increased self awareness and insight	39	40
Increased my respect and liking for other women	24	24
I am a happier person	31	31
I feel tired and depressed	2	1
I have become more open to new ideas and people	36	37

27. During your participation in the program, which of the following has occurred?

	P	A
Family has less time together	22	30
Family has become more self-reliant and organized	32	42
Family has become closer, talk things over more	34	37
Marital tensions and difficulties	13	18
Marital relations improved, greater rapport with spouse	35	37
My children's respect and regard toward me has increased	54	61
My children are upset and resent my involvement	4	4
Has improved my status on the job	34	39
Co-workers disapprove of or resent my involvement	8	5
Less time for social life	35	38
Other people respect me more	51	53
Some friends or neighbors are disapproving or jealous	11	17

28. Indicate which of the following have been very supportive of your decision to contact or participate in the program.

	P	A
Husband	62	57
Children	43	39
Mother	32	30

Father	25	23
Siblings	27	25
Women friends	49	43
Men friends	29	27
Employer	36	34
Relatives	20	17
Faculty	39	43
Program staff	44	48
Classmates	43	35
Neighbors	14	11

29. Which of the following problems has been very important during your participation in the program?

	P	A
Costs	26	28
Location, distance, transportation	26	29
Time of day classes are offered	46	46
Negative experience with instructor	8	9
Lack of self-confidence	12	10
Lack of direction or purpose	14	16
Nonsupportive family attitudes	5	6
Family obligations, including housework and children	18	19
Lack of time	20	24
Lack of energy or physical endurance	11	13
Guilt about money	9	7
Guilt about neglect of children	8	7
Job responsibilities	19	22
Lack of specific skills and abilities	15	17
Medical reasons: personal illness, family illness, pregnancy	5	6
Other _____	2	3

Below are two questions specifically designed to assess the continuing education program and its services and to provide an opportunity for recommendations.

30. Indicate your degree of overall satisfaction with the Continuing Education program.

	P	A
Very satisfied	45	43
Somewhat satisfied	36	35
Neutral	9	12
Somewhat dissatisfied	7	8
Very dissatisfied	3	2

31. On the basis of your contact and experience with the program, what changes would you recommend?

	P	A
Provide child care	11	15

Lower tuition	17	21
Provide financial aid	17	20
Improve quality of teachers and speakers	9	12
Reach and enroll wider population (men, younger women, disadvantaged women)	19	20
Increase publicity	22	19
Evaluate courses and services; follow up on participants	19	25
Have more locations	20	20
Greater variety of courses	19	23
More choice of times that services are offered	21	21
Provide for more contact among participants	12	13
Become more independent of parent institution's facilities and staff	5	4
Make counseling responsive to individual needs and differences	17	22
Increase funding and staffing of program	20	19
Provide better educational and occupational information	22	26
Provide or improve job placement	20	29

V. *The following section includes questions about some of your personal views and attitudes.*

32. How do you feel about the women's movement?

	P	A
Positively	53	50
Negatively	4	2
Mixed	43	48

33. From the list of changes given below, which characterize the ways in which you have been affected *by the women's movement?*

	P	A
I am less tolerant of women who are traditional housewives	19	17
I feel equal to men	66	62
I have raised my goals and am more ambitious	69	65
I ask the family to share more in household chores	57	61
I have been reinforced and supported for my traditional views	28	26
I question my lifestyle and goals	56	56

	P	A
I have no respect for "aggressive" feminists	25	25
I encourage girls to consider all career alternatives, including "men's" jobs	88	88
I have more respect for and understanding of women	75	74
I am more aware of issues concerning women	91	92
My marriage has improved	32	36
I feel that girls should have the option to join boys' organizations	59	56
I have greater self-esteem	65	69
I feel that men exploit women in work situations	75	75
I feel more restless and discontent with my life	33	30
My marriage has been threatened or dissolved	17	13
I have been reinforced and supported for my feminist views	47	46
Other _____	5	3

34. Indicate any ways in which you are active in the women's movement:

	P	A
National women's organizations (NOW, WEAL)	7	7
Consciousness-raising groups	15	16
Feminist meetings, conferences, or demonstrations	10	9
Women's caucuses, coalitions, special commissions	10	10
Other community, legal, or political work on behalf of women	20	20

35. How important is it for your own self-fulfillment to have a career in addition to being a wife and mother?

	P	A
Very important	52	47
Important	26	30
Neutral	14	13
Unimportant	5	7
Very unimportant	4	3

36. How old do you feel the child(ren) should be before a mother returns to school or work?

	P	A
Infancy	15	13

Ages 2-5	18	14
Age 6 (or when entering elementary school)	32	34
Ages 7-12	14	13
Ages 13-17	12	19
Age 18 or older	9	7

37. If you ever married, to what extent did you and your husband discuss *your* educational and occupational plans before you were married?

	P	A
Not at all, because it was already understood that I would *not* be continuing work or school	26	28
Not at all, because it was already understood that I *would* be continuing work or school	32	30
Somewhat	32	35
Extensively	10	8

38. If married, what is your present husband's attitude toward your working, now or in the future?

	P	A
Very approving	61	57
Somewhat approving	19	21
Neutral	13	11
Somewhat disapproving	6	8
Very disapproving	1	3

39. How would you describe your present marriage or, if unmarried, your current love relationship?

	P	A
No current relationship	14	11
Very happy	43	42
Fairly happy	32	37
Not too happy	8	8
Very unhappy	4	2

40. Your health at the present time:

	P	A
Excellent	48	48
Very good	31	33
Good	15	13
Fair	6	5
Poor	1	1

41. Rate yourself on each of the following traits as you really think you are when compared with the average woman of your own age.

	Highest 10 percent	
	P	A
Physical appearance	17	18
Social self-confidence	13	14
Intellectual self-confidence	15	19
Sensitivity to criticism	13	9
Popularity with women	9	7
Popularity with men	9	9

Leadership ability	14	15
Academic ability	20	21
Effectiveness on the job	30	29
Homemaking ability	16	15
Success as a mother	23	22
Success as a wife	22	20
Athletic ability	6	6
Drive to achieve	21	20
Originality	17	18
Cheerfulness	16	17
Assertiveness	13	12
Mental and emotional well-being	16	19
Public speaking ability	9	11
Writing ability	15	17
Artistic ability	11	12
Mathematical ability	6	4
Independence	27	24
Physical stamina	12	17

VI. *Alumnae and current participants: If you are currently in a degree or certificate program anywhere, please answer the following questions. Alumnae: If not, please skip to question 57. Current participants: If not, you have completed the questionnaire. Thank you for your help.*

42. What is the relationship between your certificate or degree program and the Continuing Education program?

	P	A
There is no connection	39	62
Continuing Education plans and administers the program	36	6
Continuing Education suggested or placed me in an existing program run by the parent institution	19	22
Continuing Education referred me to an existing program at another institution	7	9

43. For how long have you been in the degree of certificate program?

	P	A
Less than 1 month	6	2
Less than 3 months	25	11
Less than 1 year	40	23
1-2 years	14	41
More than 2 years	16	23

44. What are your degree plans?

	Degree working toward		Highest degree hoped for	
	P	A	P	A
Certificate	24	13	8	4
Associate of Arts degree	8	8	2	0
Bachelor's	49	38	17	19
Master's	15	35	45	45
Doctorate (PhD, EdD)	4	5	18	23
Professional (MD, DDS, LLB, JD)	1	2	11	10

45. What is your major field of study?

	P	A
Arts and humanities	16	18
Business (merchandising, business administration	9	10
Education	11	15
General studies or liberal arts	7	7
Health fields—non-MD (nursing, home economics, recreation)	8	9
Medicine, dentistry, law	3	4
Natural sciences and mathematics	3	1
Social sciences (social work, sociology, psychology, economics)	22	26
Legal paraprofessional	11	1
Other paraprofessional fields (landscape architect assistant, editing and publications, counseling specialist)	6	2
Women's studies	1	2
Other _____	4	6

46. What is your grade point average?

	P	A
A	26	38
B	47	42
C	5	7
Below C	0	0
I have received no grades	22	13

47. Do you have any concerns about your ability to finance your education/training?

	P	A
None (I am confident that I will have sufficient funds)	36	47
Some concern (but I will probably have enough funds)	44	39
Major concern (not sure I will have enough funds to complete it)	21	13

48. Indicate the major sources for financing your education/training.

	P	A
Employer	14	10
Spouse	44	52
Loan	9	10
Part-time job or full-time job	32	22
Scholarship or fellowship	16	10
Family (parents, other relatives)	10	4
Savings, investments	19	13
Insurance, pension, social security, retirement benefits, alimony	4	4

Trust fund, inheritance, gifts	5	5

49. Which of the following personal qualities have been very important in contributing to your progress in the program?

	P	A
Perseverance, determination	75	80
Ambition	60	65
Desire to learn	82	84
Assertiveness	35	38
Self-confidence	40	44
Realistic self-assessment, self-awareness	54	59
Self-discipline and organization	57	59
Adaptability	51	58
Intelligence and related aptitudes	52	60
Other _____	4	5

50. Indicate which of the following are very important in choosing your field:

	P	A
Intrinsic interest in field	74	74
Job opportunities	31	33
Prior job or educational experiences	30	34
Prior personal experience (child-rearing, contacts with counselors, etc.)	31	30
It suits my abilities and personality	62	71
Can afford the educational and training costs	17	24
Length of time in preparation is relatively short	18	18

51. Are you enrolled:

	P	A
Full-time	32	35
Part-time	68	65

52. Do you prefer:

	P	A
Full-time	39	38
Part-time	44	50
Either way	17	13

53. What aspects of the academic work create particular pressures or anxieties for you?

	P	A
Exams	62	66
Conflicting demands on my time (home, school, job)	72	74
Lengthy homework assignments	49	44
Writing (papers, assignments)	46	52

Speaking before a class or group	31	36
Reading concentration, comprehension, or recall	34	36
Inadequate preparation in math and science	34	42
Grades; evaluation	38	34
Some instructors' attitudes	28	33
Some instructors' ways of presenting subject matter	43	41
Inadequate study skills	27	25
Other _____	5	5

Current participants: This completes the questionnaire. Thank you very much for your help.

Alumnae: If you were affiliated with a degree or certificate program during the time you were a participant of the continuing education program for women, please answer questions 57-63. If not, skip to question 64.

54. For how long were you in the degree or certificate program?
    Less than one month 2
    Less than 3 months 9
    Less than 1 academic year 24
    1-2 years 32
    More than 2 years 33

55. At that time, what were your degree plans?

	Degree Working Toward	Highest Degree Hoped For
Certificate	36	16
Associate of Arts degree	5	3
Bachelor's	41	24
Master's	16	39
Doctorate (PhD, EdD)	2	12
Professional (MD, DDS, LLB, JD)	0	7

56. What was your major field of study?
    Arts and humanities 19
    Business (merchandising, business administration 4
    Education 13
    General studies or liberal arts 13
    Health fields—non-MD (nursing, home economics, recreation) 5
    Medicine, law, dentistry 1
    Natural sciences and mathematics 2
    Social sciences (social work, sociology, psychology, economics) 15
    Legal paraprofessional 21
    Other paraprofessional fields (landscape architect assistant, editing and publications, counseling specialist) 2

Women's studies 2
Other _____ 3

57. What was your grade average?
A 32
B 50
C 8
Below C 0
I have received no grades 11

58. Were you enrolled:
Full-time 39
Part-time 60

59. Which of the following were important sources for financing your education/training.

	Major source	Minor source	Not a source
Employer	11	4	85
Spouse	46	5	48
Loan	12	7	81
Part-time job or full-time job	20	17	63
Scholarship or fellowship	11	4	85
Family (parents, other relatives)	10	8	82
Savings, investments	18	12	70
Insurance, pension, social security, retirement benefits, alimony	1	1	98
Trust fund, inheritance, gifts	8	1	91

60. Did you receive the degree or certificate you were working toward?
Yes 76
No 24

61. If you are *not* working or in school now, are you:

	Yes	No
Planning to take courses	71	29
Planning to enroll in a degree program	33	67
Looking for a paid full-time job	15	85
Looking for a paid part-time job	23	77
Working in volunteer positions	47	53
Staying home with your family	54	46

62. If you are not currently taking courses and/or do not plan to continue taking courses next year, please circle your one primary reason:
Have already completed my degree or training 24
No interest in further education or training 3
Insufficient interest in specific course offerings or in the field 7

Dissatisfaction with the program structure or administration	4
Academic problems or fears	2
Length of time required to get degree or certificate (too long)	5
Desire to work	15
Enjoyment of staying at home, tending house	4
Husband's objections or preferences	1
Difficulties and costs of household maintenance and child care	3
Children's needs or preferences; pregnancy	6
Illness (personal or family) or death	4
Costs, financial need	5
Indecision about goals	11
Other	7

This completes the questionnaire. Thank you very much for your help.

References

References

Allen, L. "The Council's Interest." In O. D. David, (ed., *The Education of Women: Signs for the Future*. Washington, D.C.: American Council on Education, 1959. Pp. 3–5.

Astin, A. W., and others. *The American Freshman: National Norms for Fall 1974*. Los Angeles: Cooperative Institutional Research Program, American Council on Education and the University of California at Los Angeles, 1974.

Astin, H. S. *The Woman Doctorate in America*. New York: Russell Sage Foundation, 1969.

Ballmer, H., and Cozby, P. C. "Changes in Family Relationships When the Wife Returns to College." Paper presented at the Western Psychological Association Meeting, Sacramento, California, April 25, 1975.

Baruch, R. "The Achievement Motive in Women: Implications for Career Development." *Journal of Personality and Social Psychology*, 1967, *5* (3), 260–267.

Bernard, J. *Academic Women*. University Park: Pennsylvania State University Press, 1964.

———."The Paradox of the Happy Marriage." In V. Gornick and K. Moran, eds., *Women in Sexist Society*. New York: Basic Books, 1971[a]. Pp. 85–98.

———.*Women and the Public Interest: An Essay on Policy and Protest*. Chicago: Aldine, 1971[b].

———. *The Future of Marriage*. New York: World, 1972.

———.*Women, Wives, Mothers: Values and Options*. Chicago, Aldine, 1975.

Boston Women's Health Book Collective. *Our Bodies, Ourselves*. New York: Simon and Schuster, 1971.

Brandenberg, J. B. "The Needs of Women Returning to School." *Personnel and Guidance Journal*, 1974, *53* (1), 11–18.

Brim, O. G., Jr. "Selected Theories of the Male Mid-Life Crisis: A Comparative Analysis." Paper presented at The American Psychological Association Annual Convention, New Orleans, August, 1974.

Bunting, M. "Education: A Nurturant If Not a Determinant of Professional Success." In R. B. Kundsin, ed., *Women and Success: The Anatomy of Achievement*. New York: Morrow, 1973. Pp. 208–13.

Campbell, J. W. "Women Drop Back in: Educational Innovation in the Sixties." In A. S. Rossi and A. Calderwood, eds., *Academic Women on the Move*. New York: Russell Sage Foundation, 1973. Pp. 93–124.

Carnegie Foundation for the Advancement of Teaching. *More Than Survival: Prospects for Higher Education in a Period of Uncertainty*. San Francisco: Jossey-Bass, 1975.

Commission on Non-Traditional Study. *Diversity by Design.* San Francisco: Jossey-Bass, 1973.

Continuing Education of Women. Syracuse, N. Y.: Joint Publication of ERIC Clearinghouse on Adult Education and Adult Education Association of the U.S.A. Sept. 1970.

Crosman, A. M., and Gustav, A. "Academic Success of Older People." *Psychology in the Schools,* July 1966, *3* (3), 256–258.

Durchholz, P., and O'Connor, J. "Why Women Go Back to College." *Change,* Oct. 1973, *5* (8), 52ff.

Erikson, E. H. *Childhood and Society.* rev. ed., New York: W. W. Norton, 1963.

Flavell, J. "Cognitive Changes in Adulthood." In L. R. Goulet and P. B. Baltes, eds., *Lifespan Developmental Psychology.* New York: Academic Press, 1970. Pp. 247–253.

Furlong, J. E. "A Catholic View of the Education of Women." Paper presented at conference on the Present Status and Prospective Trends of Research on the Education of Women, sponsored by the American Council on Education, Rye, New York, Oct. 27–30, 1957.

Gass, J. R. "Recurrent Education: The Issues." In S. J. Mushkin, ed., *Recurrent Education.* Washington, D. C.: National Institute of Education, Department of Health, Education and Welfare, 1973. Pp. 13–17.

Ginzberg, E. and others. *Life Styles of Educated Women.* New York: Columbia University Press, 1966.

Glick, P. C. "A Demographer Looks at American Families." *Journal of Marriage and the Family.* Feb. 1975, 15–25.

Gove, W. "The Relationship Between Sex Roles, Marital Status, and Mental Health." *Social Forces.* Sept. 1972, *51,* 34–44.

Halfter, I. "The Comparative Academic Achievement of Women." *Adult Education,* 1962, *12* (2), 106–115.

Hoffman, L. W. "Effects of Maternal Employment on the Child: A Review of the Research." *Developmental Psychology,* 1974, *10* (2), 204–228.

Horner, M. "Research Trends and Needs in Women's Education and Career Development." Occasional Paper No. 1 (edited by Helen Astin) presented at meeting of National Coalition for Research on Women's Education and Development, sponsored by Johnson Foundation at Wingspread, Racine, Wisconsin, June 1974.

Howe, F. "Sexual Stereotypes and the Public Schools." In R. B. Kundsin, ed., *Women and Success: The Anatomy of Achievement.* New York: Morrow, 1973. Pp. 123–128.

Hunter, K. "Help Women Plan for the Second Half." *Adult Leadership,* May 1965, *13,* 10.

Johnstone, J. W. C., and Rivera, R. J. *Volunteers for Learning: A Study of the Educational Pursuits of American Adults.* Chicago: Aldine, 1965.

Kahne, H. "Employment Prospects and Academic Policies." In R. B. Kundsin, ed., *Women and Success: The Anatomy of Achievement.* New York: Morrow, 1973. Pp. 160–170.

Katz, J. "Coeducational Living: Effects Upon Male-Female Relationships." In D. A. DeCoster and P. Mable, eds., *Student Development and Education in College Residence Halls.* Washington, D.C.: American College Personnel Association, 1974.

Kline, C. M. "Educational Planning for Mature Women." In S. J. Mushkin, ed., *Recurrent Education.* Washington, D. C.: National Institute of Education, 1973. Pp. 165–175.

LeBaron H. R. "An Evaluation of Home Economics Training." In O. D. David, ed., *The Education of Women: Signs for the Future.* Washington, D. C.: American Council on Education, 1959. Pp. 108–112.

London, J. "The Continuing Education of Women: A Challenge for Our Society." *Adult Leadership,* May 1966, *14,* 10.

Lowenthal, M. F., and Chiriboga, D. "Social Stress and Adaptation: Toward a Life-Course Perspective." In D. Eisdorfer and M. P. Lawton, eds., *Psychology of Adult Development and Aging.* Washington, D. C.: American Psychological Association, 1973.

Mattfeld, J. A. "A Decade of Continuing Education: Dead End or Open Door." Unpublished manuscript. Brown University, 1971. (Quoted with permission of author.)

Mulligan, K. L. *A Question of Opportunity: Women and Continuing Education.* Washington, D. C.: National Advisory Council on Extension and Continuing Education, March 1973.

Neugarten, B. L., and others. *Personality in Middle and Late Life.* New York: Atherton, 1964.

Neugarten, B. L. "Personality Change in Late Life: A Developmental Perspective." In C. Eisdorfer and M. P. Lawton, eds., *The Psychology of Adult Development and Aging.* Washington, D. C.: American Psychological Association, 1973.

Norwood, J. "The Policy Issues: Can We Agree on Goals and How Do We Get There?" Paper presented at conference on Occupational Segregation, Wellesley College, May 1975.

Oltman, R. M. *Campus 1970: Where Do Women Stand?* Research Report of a Survey of Women in Academe. December 1970. Available from the American Association of University Women.

Oppenheimer, V. K. *The Female Labor Force in the United States: Demographic and Economic Factors Governing its Growth and Changing Composition.* Population Monograph Series No. 5. Berkeley: Institute of International Studies, University of California, 1970.

O'Toole, J. "The Reserve Army of the Underemployed: I — The World of Work." *Change,* May 1975, *7* (4), 26–33ff.

Parelman, A. "Family Attitudes Toward the Student Mother As Compared With Family Attitudes Toward Working Mothers: A Pilot Study." Unpublished manuscript. Psychology Department, University of California at Los Angeles, 1974.

Rehn, G. "Towards Flexibility in Working Life." In S. J. Mushkin, ed., *Recurrent Education.* Washington, D. C.: National Institute of Education, 1973, Pp. 177–185.

Safilios-Rothschild, C. "Dual Linkages Between the Occupational and Family System: A Macrosociological Analysis." Paper presented at conference on Occupational Segregation, Wellesley College, May 1975.

Scates, A. Y. "Women Moving Ahead." *American Education,* 1966, *2* (3), 1–4.

Schletzer, V. M., and others. *Continuing Education of Women: A Five-Year Report of the Minnesota Plan.* Minneapolis: University of Minnesota, 1967.

Schwartz, F. "Women and Employers: Their Related Needs and Attitudes." In R. B. Kundsin, ed., *Woman and Success: The Anatomy of Achievement.* New York: Morrow, 1973. Pp. 178–182.

Simon, A. "Emotional Problems of Women: Mature Years and Beyond." *Psychosomatics,* 1968, *9,* Vol. 4, 12–16.

Sklar, J. and Berkov, B. "The American Birth Rate: Evidences of a Coming Rise." *Science,* August 1975, *189,* Pp. 693–700.

Steinman, A., and Fox, D. J. "Male-Female Perceptions of the Female Role in the United States." *Journal of Psychology,* 1966, *64,* 265–76.

Sutherland, R. L. "Some Basic Facts." In O. D. David, ed., *The Education of Women: Signs for the Future.* Washington, D. C.: American Council on Education, 1959. Pp. 14–16.

Tough, A. *Why Adults Learn: A Study of the Major Reasons for Beginning and Continuing a Learning Project.* Monographs in Adult Education No. 3. Toronto: Department of Adult Education, Ontario Institute for Studies in Education, 1968.

U. S. Department of Commerce, Bureau of the Census. *Characteristics of American Youth.* Current Population Reports, Special Studies, No. 51. Washington, D. C.: Government Printing Office, 1974.

U. S. Department of Labor, Employment Standards Administration, Women's Bureau. *Continuing Education Programs and Services for Women.* Pamphlet No. 10, rev. ed., Washington, D. C.: Government Printing Office, 1971.

U. S. Department of Labor, Employment Standards Administration, Women's Bureau. *Continuing Education for Women: Current Developments.* Washington D. C.: Government Printing Office, 1974.

U. S. Department of Labor, National Manpower Council, 1962.

Vermilye, D. W., ed., *Lifelong Learners: A New Clientele for Higher Education*. San Francisco: Jossey-Bass, 1974.

Washington Post, "The Cost of a College Education." May 12, 1975.

Westervelt, E. M. *Barriers to Women's Participation in Postsecondary Education: A Review of Research and Commentaries as of 1973–74*. Washington, D. C.: Government Printing Office, 1975.

Zinberg, D. "College: When the Future Becomes the Present." In R. B. Kundsin, ed., *Women and Success: The Anatomy of Achievement*. New York: Morrow, 1973. Pp. 129–137.

Index

Index

AFL-CIO Women's Council, 15
Academic Women on the Move, 141
Adams, Arthur, 3, 4
Adams, Elizabeth Kemper, 139
Admission procedures, institutes of higher education, 52–53
"Adult Development and Education," 45–56
Alumnae, active, 78–79
American Association of University Women, 14, 17
American Council on Education (ACE), 3, 4, 15, 139–45
Anderson, Florence, 8
Antioch College, 9
Astin, Helen S., 45–56, 57–88, 135, 175

Ballmer, H., and P.C. Cozby, 103
Banning, Margaret C., 140
Barnard College, 16
Baruch, R., 46
Bernard, Jessie, 109–24
Berry, Jane, 141
"Birth of an Idea: An Account of the Genesis of Women's Continuing Education, The," 1–21
Boston Women's Health Book Collective, 121
Brandenberg, J.B., 52, 54
Brown University, 16
Brownlee, Jean, 13
Bryn Mawr, 17
Buddhism, seminar, 27
Bunting, Mary I., 2, 10, 11, 117, 140

Campbell, Jean, 141
Career Potential Workshops, 28
Carnegie Commission, 19
Carnegie Corporation, 5, 7, 8, 11, 14, 48, 125, 142
Case-study program, CEW, 23–41; organization of, 31–34; relation to CEW, 34–36; self-assessment, 36–41
"Case-Study Programs: Academic Misfits Which Lasted, The" 23–41
Center for Continuing Education, Sarah Lawrence College, 6, 12, 17
Center for Educational Research and Innovation, 47–48
Center for the Study of Liberal Education for Adults, 9n
Charles E. Merrill Trust, 11
Children, effects of CEW on, 100–102
Claremont University, 17
Clarenbach, Kathryn, 14–15

Clearinghouse on Adult Education, Syracuse University, 18
Cless, Elizabeth L., 1–21, 114, 115
College entrance tests, 52–53
Commission on the Education of Women, ACE, 1, 3–4, 15, 139, 140–141, 142
Commission on Women in Higher Education, 5
Committee on Training Women for the Professions, ACE, 3
Committee on Training of Women for Professional Service, 139
Comprehensive Health Manpower Act, 142
Conference on the Present Status and Prospective Trends of Research on the Education of Women, 1957, 141
Consciousness-raising, 15
Contemporary Issues, seminar, 27
Continuing education for women (CEW), 3, 7, 8, 18–21, 23, 24–26, 31–41, 49–56; future of, 107–28; home life of women in, 89–105; profile of women in, 57–88; programs of, 27–30
Conversation skills for women, 28
Counseling, 55, 56
"Counseling Girls: High School and College," 142
Current Information Services on the Continuing Education of Women, 18

David, Opal, 4, 140, 141
Dean, John, 141
Demographic characteristics, women in continuing education, 58–61
Dolan, Eleanor, 51
Donlon, Mary H., 139
Durchholz, P., and J. O'Connor, 53

Economy, impact of on continuing education, 115–17
Education Amendment, 1972, 142
Education and a Woman's Life, 4, 142
"Education of Women, The," 142
"Education of Women: Signs for the Future, The," 141
Educational Record, 139
Educational Resources Information Center, 18
Educational status, women in continuing education, 61–68
Ellis Phillips Foundation, 140
"Empty nest" syndrome, 19
Equal Employment Opportunity Act, 142
Equal Employment Opportunity Task Force, 143

177

Equal Pay Act, 1963, 142
Equal Rights Amendment Coalition, 15
Equal Rights Amendment, CEW and,
    118–19
Europe, 120
Executive Challenge: The Woman Admin-
    istrator, 28
Executive Order 11246, 142
Existentialism and Contemporary Ethics,
    seminar, 27
"Exploration of the Needs of Freshman and
    Sophomore Women College Students
    for Life Planning, An," 141

Families, women in continuing education
    and, 43–105
Feminism, 2, 20
Flexitime, 120–21
Ford Foundation, 8
Frequency Distributions, 147–65
Fried, Frank, Harris, Shriver and Kample-
    man, 143
Friedan, Betty, 1, 2
Funding, 25
Furlong, J.E., 1

Gannon, Sister Ann Ida, 142
Gardner, John, 8
Gildersleeve, Virginia, 142
Ginzberg, Eli, 20
Glick, Paul, 109–10
Goddard College, 19
Goucher College, 17
Gould, Samuel, 31
Graduate school. See Continuing education
    for women
Growing Up Female, 28
Guilt, 51–52

Habein, Margaret, 140
Halfter, I., 20
Harris, Patricia Roberts, 143
Harvard University, 7
Henderson, Virginia, 13
Heyns, Roger, 5, 143
Hill, Reuben, 122
"Historical Notes on the American Council
    of Education's Involvement with the
    Concerns of Women in Higher Edu-
    cation," 139–45
Hoffman, Lois, 104
Hogg Foundation for Mental Hygiene, 1
Horner, Matina, 116, 117
Hottel, Althea, 140
How Fare American Women?, 4, 140
Howe, Florence, 119
Husbands, attitudes of toward women in
    continuing education, 94–100

Intercollegiate Association of Women Stu-
    dents, 141–42
Itasca Conference, 142
Invitational Seminar on Identification, Rec-
    ommendation, and Placement of
    Women in Higher Education Admin-
    istration, 144

Jackson College, 17
Jackson, Priscilla, 15
Jahoda, Marie, 141
Japan, 120
Johnson Foundation, 15
Johnstone, J.W.C., and R.J. Rivera, 48–49
Josiah Macy, Jr. Foundation, 11
Junior League, 28, 32

Kahne, Hilda, 115–16
Katz, Joseph, 16, 89–105, 119, 135
Kellog Foundation, 8, 15
Kennedy, John F., 14
Korean War, 139

League of Women Voters, 32
Leland, Carole, 23–41, 135
Life Styles of Educated Women, 20
Liveright, A.A., 9n
Lloyd-Jones, Esther, 2, 6, 140, 141
Los Angeles, Calif., 138
Loyola University, 17
Lunch and Learn, 28

McBride, Katherine, 141, 142
Married women students, 90–93. See also
    Families, women in continuing edu-
    cation and
Martin, Gertrude, 139
Maslow, 15
Mattfield, Jacquelyn, 16, 17, 18, 49
Mental health, CEW and, 117–18
Merry, Margaret Habein, 4
Mill, John Stuart, 1
Mills, 17
Minnesota Plan for the Continuing Educa-
    tion of Women, 6, 8–10, 12, 13–14, 17
Morrill Act, 19–20
Mortar Board Association, 13
Mulligan, K.L., 49, 53–54

National Association of Women Deans,
    Administrators, and Counselors, 140
National Association of Women Deans and
    Counselors, 3
National Coalition for Research on
    Women's Education and Develop-
    ment, 15–16
National Commission on the Status of
    Women, 14

National Institutes of Health, 141
"National Survey of Women in Continuing Education Programs," 137–38
New Careers in Community Services, 29
New Patterns of Employment, 29
Newman Task Force, 19
Night school, 54
Noble, Jeanne, 141
Norwood, Janet, 116
Nurse Training Amendments Act, 1971, 142

Oakland University Continuum Center, 15
Occupational status, women in continuing education, 68–72
Office of Leadership Development in Higher Education, 144
Office of Women in Higher education, 143–44
Oltman, R.M., 17, 18
Oppenheimer, Valerie, 92
Organization for Economic Cooperation and Development, 47–48
O'Toole, James, 116
Our Bodies, Ourselves, 121

Pan American International Committee for Women, 139
Parelman, Allison, 103–104
Parent Participation, 28
Park, Marion, 139
Pennington, Jean, 15
Personal Growth for Women, 28
Peterson, Martha, 13, 14, 142, 143
Philadelphia, Pa., 13
Phillips, Kathryn, 140
Pifer, Alan, 8
Princeton University, 17
"Profile of the Women in Continuing Education, A," 57–88
Program A, CEW, 27–28
Program B, CEW, 28–29
Program C, CEW, 29–30
Program for Women Physicians, 11
"Psychological Problems of Women in Different Social Roles: An Exploratory Case Study," 141
Public Health Service Act, 142
Purdue University, 17

Racine, Wisc., 15
Radcliffe College, 4, 6, 7, 17, 113
Radcliffe Institute for Independent Study, 6, 10–12, 17
Raushenbush, Esther, 7, 12, 24
Rehn, Gosta, 121
Rockefeller Brothers Fund, 25
Rossi, Alice, and Ann Calderwood, 141

Safilios-Rothschild, Constantina, 120–21
Sample and procedures, 131–38
Sarah Lawrence Center for Continuing Education, 6, 12, 17
Sarah Lawrence College, 4, 6, 7, 16, 17, 113
Schletzer, Vera, 10
Schlossberg, Dr. Nancy, 143
School Counselor, The, 142
Schwartz, Felice, 13, 16, 114
Scott, Anne Firor, 16
"Self-actualization," 15
Self-ratings and attitudes, women in continuing education, 72–79
Senders, Virginia, 9–10
Separated and divorced women students, 102
Sex discrimination, 142
Single Woman in a Couple's Society, The, 28
Smith, Alice K., 11
Smith, Constance, 11
"Social and Cultural Factors Affecting Role-Conflict and Adjustment Among American Women," 141
"Some Values of Progressive Education for Women," 139
Soviet Union, 1
Span of a Woman's Life and Learning, A, 4, 142
Sputnik, 1
Steinem, Gloria, 1
Storer, Sue, 141
Student Counseling Bureau, University of Minnesota, 9
"Study of the Concerns of a Selected Group of Unmarried Women, A," 141
"Study of What Negro Women College Graduates Think of Their College Education, A," 141
Suffrage, for women, 2
Sutherland, Robert L., 1–2
Syracuse University, 17

Taylor, Dr. Emily, 143
Temple University, 17
Threinen, Constance, 14
Title I, Higher Education Act, 1965, 25
Title VII, Civil Rights Act, 1964, 142
Titles VII and VIII, Public Health Service Act, 142
Title IX, Education Amendments, 1972, 142, 143
"Togetherness," 2
Tufts University, 17
Twin Oaks commune, Va., 122

University of Kansas, 143
University of Michigan, 16
University of Minnesota, 4, 6, 7, 8–10, 113

University of Oklahoma, 19
University of Pennsylvania, 13
University of Wisconsin, 13, 14

Vassar College, 17

Washington Area Feminist Theatre, 122
Washington University, 15
Wayne State University, 143
Wellesley College, 17
Westerwelt, Esther, 16, 118–19
Whiteside, Helen, 141
Why no College?, 28
Williams, Robin, 141
Wilson, Logan, 4, 5
Wisconsin, 14
Wisconsin Tribal Women, 15
Wollstonecraft, Mary, 1
Woman Manager, The, 28
Woman Supervisor, The, 28
Women in continuing education: demo-
    graphic characteristics of, 58–61; ed-
    ucational status of, 61–68; experi-
    ences of in programs, 80–87; home
    life of, 89–94; husbands' attitudes
    toward, 94–100; occupational status
    of, 68–72; satisfaction of with pro-

grams, 87–88; self-ratings and atti-
    tudes of, 72–79
Women in the Defense Decade, 3, 139
Women in Higher Education, 142
Women: A Historical Perspective, 28
Women's Bureau, U.S. Department of
    Labor, 5, 16, 18, 49, 113
"Women's Continuing Education: Whither
    Bound?", 109–24
Women's Educational Equity Act, 143
Women's movement, 14, 75–76
Women's Political Caucus, 15
Women's Resource Center, University of
    Kansas, 143
Women's Resource Service, 29
Women in School and at Work, 29
Workshop on Freeing Sex Roles for New
    Careers, 144
Workshop for Women Considering Careers
    in College and University Admin-
    istration, 144
World War II, 8, 139

Yale University, 10, 17

Zinberg, Dorothy, 116

About the Contributors

Jessie Bernard, Scholar-in-Residence at the United States Civil Rights Commission, Washington, D.C. and Professor Research Scholar Honoris Causa, Pennsylvania State University.

Elizabeth Cless, Past Director, Special Academic programs and director of Center of Continuing Education, Clarement Colleges from 1966-75.

Joseph Katz, Director of the Research Group for Human Development and Educational Policy and Professor of Human Development at the State University of New York at Stony Brook.

Carole Leland, Professor of Social Science, Laguardia Community College CUNY.

About the Editor

Helen S. Astin is Professor of Higher Education at the Graduate School of Education at UCLA, and vice-president of the Higher Education Research Institute. Previously, she was Director of Research and Education for the University Research Corporation in Washington, D.C. Her research interests are in the fields of educational progress and career development with an emphasis on women.

Helen Astin has been Chairperson of the American Psychological Association's Task Force on the Status of Women in Psychology and President of Division 35 (Division of the Psychology of Women) of the American Psychological Association. Currently she is serving on the Association's Board for Policy and Planning. She is a member of the National Research Council-Board on Human-Resource Data and Analyses, and a Trustee of Hampshire College. She serves on the Editorial Boards of the *Journal of Counseling Psychology, Journal of Vocational Behavior, Psychology of Women Quarterly, Signs,* and *Sage Annuals in Women's Policy Studies.*

Among Helen Astin's publications are: *Human Resources and Higher Education* (with Folger and Bayer); *The Woman Doctorate in America; Women: A Bibliography on Their Education and Careers* (with Suniewick and Dweck); *Higher Education and the Disadvantaged Student* (with A. W. Astin, Bisconti, and Frankel); *Open Admissions at CUNY* (with Rossmann, A. W. Astin, and El-Khawas); *Sex Roles: An Annotated Research Bibliography* (with Parelman, and Fisher); and *The Power of Protest* (with A. W. Astin, Bayer, and Bisconti).

Related Lexington Books

Edwards, Carl, *All the Tomorrows,* In Press

Lyle, Jerolyn R. and Ross, Jane, *Women in Industry,* 192 pp., 1973

Madden, Janice F., *The Economics of Sex Discrimination,* 160 pp., 1973

Murphy, Irene L., *Public Policy on the Status of Women,* 144 pp., 1973

Simon, Rita James, *Women and Crime,* 144 pp., 1975

Simmons, Adele; Freedman, Ann; Dunkle, Margaret; and Blau, Francine, *Exploitation from 9 to 5,* 224 pp., 1975

Tsuchigane, Robert and Dodge, Norton T., *Economic Discrimination Against Women in the U.S.,* 176 pp., 1974

Walker, Marsha J. and Brodsky, Stanley L., *Sexual Assault: The Victim and the Rapist,* 208 pp., 1976